MznLnx

Missing Links Exam Preps

Exam Prep for

International Marketing

Czinkota & Ronkainen, 8th Edition

The MznLnx Exam Prep is your link from the texbook and lecture to your exams.
The MznLnx Exam Preps are unauthorized and comprehensive reviews of your textbooks.

All material provided by MznLnx and Rico Publications (c) 2010
Textbook publishers and textbook authors do not particpate in or contribute to these reviews.

MznLnx

Rico
Publications

Exam Prep for International Marketing
8th Edition
Czinkota & Ronkainen

Publisher: Raymond Houge
Assistant Editor: Michael Rouger
Text and Cover Designer: Lisa Buckner
Marketing Manager: Sara Swagger
Project Manager, Editorial Production: Jerry Emerson
Art Director: Vernon Lowerui

Product Manager: Dave Mason
Editorial Asitant: Rachel Guzmanji
Pedagogy: Debra Long
Cover Image: Jim Reed/Getty Images
Text and Cover Printer: City Printing, Inc.
Compositor: Media Mix, Inc.

(c) 2010 Rico Publications
ALL RIGHTS RESERVED. No part of this work covered by the copyright may be reproduced or used in any form or by an means--graphic, electronic, or mechanical, including photocopying, recording, taping, Web distribution, information storage, and retrieval systems, or in any other manner--without the written permission of the publisher.

Printed in the United States
ISBN:

For more information about our products, contact us at:
Dave.Mason@RicoPublications.com

For permission to use material from this text or product, submit a request online to:
Dave.Mason@RicoPublications.com

Contents

CHAPTER 1
The Global Marketing Imperative — 1

CHAPTER 2
Trade Institutions and Trade Policy — 4

CHAPTER 3
The Cultural Environment — 7

CHAPTER 4
The Economic Environment — 12

CHAPTER 5
The Political and Legal Environment — 21

CHAPTER 6
Strategic Planning — 26

CHAPTER 7
Marketing Organization, Implementation, and Control — 30

CHAPTER 8
Research — 34

CHAPTER 9
Market Entry and Expansion — 42

CHAPTER 10
Product Adaptation — 48

CHAPTER 11
Export Pricing — 53

CHAPTER 12
Marketing Communication — 58

CHAPTER 13
Distribution Management — 64

CHAPTER 14
Global Product Management and Branding — 69

CHAPTER 15
Global Services — 73

CHAPTER 16
Global Logistics and Materials Management — 77

CHAPTER 17
Global Pricing — 82

CHAPTER 18
Global Promotional Strategies — 85

ANSWER KEY — 93

TO THE STUDENT

COMPREHENSIVE

The *MznLnx* Exam Prep series is designed to help you pass your exams. Editors at MznLnx review your textbooks and then prepare these practice exams to help you master the textbook material. Unlike study guides, workbooks, and practice tests provided by the texbook publisher and textbook authors, *MznLnx* gives you **all** of the material in each chapter in exam form, not just samples, so you can be sure to nail your exam.

MECHANICAL

The MznLnx Exam Prep series creates exams that will help you learn the subject matter as well as test you on your understanding. Each question is designed to help you master the concept. Just working through the exams, you gain an understanding of the subject--its a simple mechanical process that produces success.

INTEGRATED STUDY GUIDE AND REVIEW

MznLnx is not just a set of exams designed to test you, its also a comprehensive review of the subject content. Each exam question is also a review of the concept, making sure that you will get the answer correct without having to go to other sources of material. You learn as you go! Its the easiest way to pass an exam.

HUMOR

Studying can be tedious and dry. MznLnx's instructional design includes moderate humor within the exam questions on occassion, to break the tedium and revitalize the brain

Chapter 1. The Global Marketing Imperative

1. The Oxford University Press defines _____ as 'marketing on a worldwide scale reconciling or taking commercial advantage of global operational differences, similarities and opportunities in order to meet global objectives.' Oxford University Press' Glossary of Marketing Terms.

Here are three reasons for the shift from domestic to _____ as given by the authors of the textbook, _____ Management--3rd Edition by Masaaki Kotabe and Kristiaan Helsen, 2004.

One of the product categories in which global competition has been easy to track is in U.S. automotive sales.

   a. Global marketing
   b. Guerrilla Marketing
   c. Digital marketing
   d. Diversity marketing

2. _____ is defined by the American _____ Association as the activity, set of institutions, and processes for creating, communicating, delivering, and exchanging offerings that have value for customers, clients, partners, and society at large. The term developed from the original meaning which referred literally to going to market, as in shopping, or going to a market to sell goods or services.

_____ practice tends to be seen as a creative industry, which includes advertising, distribution and selling.

   a. Product naming
   b. Marketing myopia
   c. Customer acquisition management
   d. Marketing

3. A _____ is the space, actual or metaphorical, in which a market operates. The term is also used in a trademark law context to denote the actual consumer environment, ie. the 'real world' in which products and services are provided and consumed.
   a. Power III
   b. Marketplace
   c. 6-3-5 Brainwriting
   d. 180SearchAssistant

4. _____ is one of the four elements of marketing mix. An organization or set of organizations (go-betweens) involved in the process of making a product or service available for use or consumption by a consumer or business user.

The other three parts of the marketing mix are product, pricing, and promotion.

a. Japan Advertising Photographers' Association
b. Comparison-Shopping agent
c. Better Living Through Chemistry
d. Distribution

5. Human beings are also considered to be _____ because they have the ability to change raw materials into valuable _____. The term Human _____ can also be defined as the skills, energies, talents, abilities and knowledge that are used for the production of goods or the rendering of services. While taking into account human beings as _____, the following things have to be kept in mind:

- The size of the population
- The capabilities of the individuals in that population

Many _____ cannot be consumed in their original form. They have to be processed in order to change them into more usable commodities.

a. 180SearchAssistant
b. Power III
c. 6-3-5 Brainwriting
d. Resources

6. _____ is a business discipline which is focused on the practical application of marketing techniques and the management of a firm's marketing resources and activities. Marketing managers are often responsible for influencing the level, timing, and composition of customer demand accepted definition of the term. In part, this is because the role of a marketing manager can vary significantly based on a business' size, corporate culture, and industry context.

a. Door-to-door
b. Performance-based advertising
c. Business structure
d. Marketing management

7. In statistics, an _____ is a term in a statistical model added when the effect of two or more variables is not simply additive. Such a term reflects that the effect of one variable depends on the values of one or more other variables.

Thus, for a response Y and two variables x_1 and x_2 an additive model would be:

$$Y = ax_1 + bx_2 + \text{error}$$

In contrast to this,

$$Y = ax_1 + bx_2 + c(x_1 \times x_2) + \text{error},$$

is an example of a model with an _____ between variables x_1 and x_2 ('error' refers to the random variable whose value by which y differs from the expected value of y.)

a. ACNielsen
b. Interaction
c. AMAX
d. ADTECH

Chapter 2. Trade Institutions and Trade Policy

1. The Oxford University Press defines _____ as 'marketing on a worldwide scale reconciling or taking commercial advantage of global operational differences, similarities and opportunities in order to meet global objectives.' Oxford University Press' Glossary of Marketing Terms.

Here are three reasons for the shift from domestic to _____ as given by the authors of the textbook, _____ Management--3rd Edition by Masaaki Kotabe and Kristiaan Helsen, 2004.

One of the product categories in which global competition has been easy to track is in U.S. automotive sales.

  a. Global marketing
  b. Guerrilla Marketing
  c. Digital marketing
  d. Diversity marketing

2. _____ is an organization's process of defining its strategy and making decisions on allocating its resources to pursue this strategy, including its capital and people. Various business analysis techniques can be used in _____, including SWOT analysis (Strengths, Weaknesses, Opportunities, and Threats) and PEST analysis (Political, Economic, Social, and Technological analysis) or STEER analysis involving Socio-cultural, Technological, Economic, Ecological, and Regulatory factors and EPISTEL (Environment, Political, Informatic, Social, Technological, Economic and Legal)

_____ is the formal consideration of an organization's future course. All _____ deals with at least one of three key questions:

  1. 'What do we do?'
  2. 'For whom do we do it?'
  3. 'How do we excel?'

In business _____, the third question is better phrased 'How can we beat or avoid competition?'. (Bradford and Duncan, page 1.)

  a. 6-3-5 Brainwriting
  b. 180SearchAssistant
  c. Strategic planning
  d. Power III

3. _____ is defined by the American _____ Association as the activity, set of institutions, and processes for creating, communicating, delivering, and exchanging offerings that have value for customers, clients, partners, and society at large. The term developed from the original meaning which referred literally to going to market, as in shopping, or going to a market to sell goods or services.

_____ practice tends to be seen as a creative industry, which includes advertising, distribution and selling.

a. Customer acquisition management
b. Product naming
c. Marketing myopia
d. Marketing

4. _____ in organizations and public policy is both the organizational process of creating and maintaining a plan; and the psychological process of thinking about the activities required to create a desired goal on some scale. As such, it is a fundamental property of intelligent behavior. This thought process is essential to the creation and refinement of a plan, or integration of it with other plans, that is, it combines forecasting of developments with the preparation of scenarios of how to react to them.
a. 6-3-5 Brainwriting
b. Power III
c. 180SearchAssistant
d. Planning

5. The General Agreement on Tariffs and Trade was the outcome of the failure of negotiating governments to create the International Trade Organization (ITO.) _____ was formed in 1947 and lasted until 1994, when it was replaced by the World Trade Organization. The Bretton Woods Conference had introduced the idea for an organization to regulate trade as part of a larger plan for economic recovery after World War II.
a. General Agreement on Tariffs and Trade
b. Power III
c. GATT
d. Trade pact

6. The _____ is an international financial institution that provides financial and technical assistance to developing countries for development programs (e.g. bridges, roads, schools, etc.) with the stated goal of reducing poverty.

The _____ differs from the _____ Group, in that the _____ comprises only two institutions:

- International Bank for Reconstruction and Development (IBRD)
- International Development Association (IDA)

Whereas the latter incorporates these two in addition to three more:

- International Finance Corporation (IFC)
- Multilateral Investment Guarantee Agency (MIGA)
- International Centre for Settlement of Investment Disputes (ICSID)

John Maynard Keynes (right) represented the UK at the conference, and Harry Dexter White represented the US.

Chapter 2. Trade Institutions and Trade Policy

The _____ was created following the ratification of the United Nations Monetary and Financial Conference of the Bretton Woods agreement. The concept was originally conceived in July 1944 at the United Nations Monetary and Financial Conference.

a. Power III
b. 180SearchAssistant
c. 6-3-5 Brainwriting
d. World Bank

7. _____s is the social science that studies the production, distribution, and consumption of goods and services. The term _____s comes from the Ancient Greek οἰκονομία from οἶκος (oikos, 'house') + νόμος (nomos, 'custom' or 'law'), hence 'rules of the house(hold)'. Current _____ models developed out of the broader field of political economy in the late 19th century, owing to a desire to use an empirical approach more akin to the physical sciences.

a. Industrial organization
b. ACNielsen
c. ADTECH
d. Economic

8. An economic and _____ is a single market with a common currency. It is to be distinguished from a mere currency union, which does not involve a single market. This is the fifth stage of economic integration.

a. Geographical pricing
b. Zone pricing
c. Monetary Union
d. Competitive

9. _____ is exchange of capital, goods, and services across international borders or territories. In most countries, it represents a significant share of gross domestic product (GDP.) While _____ has been present throughout much of history, its economic, social, and political importance has been on the rise in recent centuries.

a. Incoterms
b. ACNielsen
c. ADTECH
d. International Trade

Chapter 3. The Cultural Environment

1. The Oxford University Press defines _____ as 'marketing on a worldwide scale reconciling or taking commercial advantage of global operational differences, similarities and opportunities in order to meet global objectives.' Oxford University Press' Glossary of Marketing Terms.

   Here are three reasons for the shift from domestic to _____ as given by the authors of the textbook, _____ Management--3rd Edition by Masaaki Kotabe and Kristiaan Helsen, 2004.

   One of the product categories in which global competition has been easy to track is in U.S. automotive sales.

   a. Digital marketing
   b. Diversity marketing
   c. Guerrilla Marketing
   d. Global marketing

2. _____ is defined by the American _____ Association as the activity, set of institutions, and processes for creating, communicating, delivering, and exchanging offerings that have value for customers, clients, partners, and society at large. The term developed from the original meaning which referred literally to going to market, as in shopping, or going to a market to sell goods or services.

   _____ practice tends to be seen as a creative industry, which includes advertising, distribution and selling.

   a. Customer acquisition management
   b. Product naming
   c. Marketing myopia
   d. Marketing

3. A _____ is the space, actual or metaphorical, in which a market operates. The term is also used in a trademark law context to denote the actual consumer environment, ie. the 'real world' in which products and services are provided and consumed.
   a. Power III
   b. Marketplace
   c. 6-3-5 Brainwriting
   d. 180SearchAssistant

Chapter 3. The Cultural Environment

4. _____ is difficult to define. For example, in 1952, Alfred Kroeber and Clyde Kluckhohn compiled a list of 164 definitions of '_____' in _____: A Critical Review of Concepts and Definitions. However, the word '_____' is most commonly used in three basic senses:

- excellence of taste in the fine arts and humanities
- an integrated pattern of human knowledge, belief, and behavior that depends upon the capacity for symbolic thought and social learning
- the set of shared attitudes, values, goals, and practices that characterizes an institution, organization or group.

When the concept first emerged in eighteenth- and nineteenth-century Europe, it connoted a process of cultivation or improvement, as in agriculture or horticulture. In the nineteenth century, it came to refer first to the betterment or refinement of the individual, especially through education, and then to the fulfillment of national aspirations or ideals.

   a. AStore
   b. African Americans
   c. Albert Einstein
   d. Culture

5. A _____ is a relatively new executive level position at a corporation, company, organization typically reporting directly to the CEO or board of directors. The _____ is responsible for a brand's image, experience, and promise, and propagating it throughout all aspects of the company. The brand officer oversees marketing, advertising, design, public relations and customer service departments.
   a. Chief brand officer
   b. Chief executive officer
   c. Financial analyst
   d. Power III

6. _____ involves disseminating information about a product, product line, brand, or company. It is one of the four key aspects of the marketing mix. (The other three elements are product marketing, pricing, and distribution). P>_____ is generally sub-divided into two parts:

- Above the line _____: Promotion in the media (e.g. TV, radio, newspapers, Internet and Mobile Phones) in which the advertiser pays an advertising agency to place the ad
- Below the line _____: All other _____. Much of this is intended to be subtle enough for the consumer to be unaware that _____ is taking place. E.g. sponsorship, product placement, endorsements, sales _____, merchandising, direct mail, personal selling, public relations, trade shows

Chapter 3. The Cultural Environment

a. Davie Brown Index
b. Bottling lines
c. Cashmere Agency
d. Promotion

7. A personal and cultural _____ is a relative ethic _____, an assumption upon which implementation can be extrapolated. A _____ system is a set of consistent _____s and measures that is soo not true. A principle _____ is a foundation upon which other _____s and measures of integrity are based.

a. Value
b. Supreme Court of the United States
c. Perceptual maps
d. Package-on-Package

8. _____ is an authority or agency in a country responsible for collecting and safeguarding _____ duties and for controlling the flow of goods including animals, personal effects and hazardous items in and out of a country. Depending on local legislation and regulations, the import or export of some goods may be restricted or forbidden, and the _____ agency enforces these rules. The _____ agency may be different from the immigration authority, which monitors persons who leave or enter the country, checking for appropriate documentation, apprehending people wanted by international arrest warrants, and impeding the entry of others deemed dangerous to the country.

a. Registered trademark symbol
b. Madrid system for the international registration of marks
c. Specific Performance
d. Customs

9. A _____ is a form of qualitative research in which a group of people are asked about their attitude towards a product, service, concept, advertisement, idea, or packaging. Questions are asked in an interactive group setting where participants are free to talk with other group members.

Ernest Dichter originated the idea of having a 'group therapy' for products and this process is what became known as a _____.

a. Focus group
b. Cross tabulation
c. Marketing research process
d. Logit analysis

10. A _____ is a sociological concept referring to a group to which an individual or another group is compared.

Chapter 3. The Cultural Environment

_____s are used in order to evaluate and determine the nature of a given individual or other group's characteristics and sociological attributes. It is the group to which the individual relates or aspires relate himself or self psychologically.

   a. Mociology
   b. Minority
   c. Power III
   d. Reference group

11. _____ is training for cross-cultural communication and experiences. Preparing people to work outside their native country (sojourner training) is one aim of _____; for example, Peace Corps volunteers complete _____ in preparation for lengthy assignments in another culture. Learning the host culture's native language is the most extensive _____
   a. Power III
   b. Cross-cultural training
   c. 6-3-5 Brainwriting
   d. 180SearchAssistant

12. _____ is an advertisement in which a particular product specifically mentions a competitor by name for the express purpose of showing why the competitor is inferior to the product naming it.

This should not be confused with parody advertisements, where a fictional product is being advertised for the purpose of poking fun at the particular advertisement, nor should it be confused with the use of a coined brand name for the purpose of comparing the product without actually naming an actual competitor. ('Wikipedia tastes better and is less filling than the Encyclopedia Galactica.')

In the 1980s, during what has been referred to as the cola wars, soft-drink manufacturer Pepsi ran a series of advertisements where people, caught on hidden camera, in a blind taste test, chose Pepsi over rival Coca-Cola.

   a. Comparative advertising
   b. GL-70
   c. Cost per conversion
   d. Heavy-up

13. _____ was a psychologist and marketing expert who is widely considered to be the 'father of motivational research.'

Chapter 3. The Cultural Environment

He received his doctorate from the University of Vienna in 1934 and emigrated with his wife Hedy (née Langfelder) to the United States in 1937. In 1946 he founded the Institute of Motivational Research in Croton-on-Hudson, New York (later moved to his home in Peekskill), and in the succeeding years founded similar institutes in Switzerland and Germany.

Dichter pioneered the application of Freudian psychoanalytic concepts and techniques to business--in particular to the study of consumer behavior in the marketplace.

   a. Andre Kirk Agassi
   b. AStore
   c. Elmer Davis
   d. Ernest Dichter

14. Human beings are also considered to be _____ because they have the ability to change raw materials into valuable _____. The term Human _____ can also be defined as the skills, energies, talents, abilities and knowledge that are used for the production of goods or the rendering of services. While taking into account human beings as _____, the following things have to be kept in mind:

   - The size of the population
   - The capabilities of the individuals in that population

Many _____ cannot be consumed in their original form. They have to be processed in order to change them into more usable commodities.

   a. 180SearchAssistant
   b. 6-3-5 Brainwriting
   c. Power III
   d. Resources

Chapter 4. The Economic Environment

1. _____ is difficult to define. For example, in 1952, Alfred Kroeber and Clyde Kluckhohn compiled a list of 164 definitions of '_____' in _____: A Critical Review of Concepts and Definitions. However, the word '_____' is most commonly used in three basic senses:

- excellence of taste in the fine arts and humanities
- an integrated pattern of human knowledge, belief, and behavior that depends upon the capacity for symbolic thought and social learning
- the set of shared attitudes, values, goals, and practices that characterizes an institution, organization or group.

When the concept first emerged in eighteenth- and nineteenth-century Europe, it connoted a process of cultivation or improvement, as in agriculture or horticulture. In the nineteenth century, it came to refer first to the betterment or refinement of the individual, especially through education, and then to the fulfillment of national aspirations or ideals.

   a. Albert Einstein
   b. African Americans
   c. AStore
   d. Culture

2. _____s is the social science that studies the production, distribution, and consumption of goods and services. The term _____s comes from the Ancient Greek οἰκονομῖα from οἴκος (oikos, 'house') + νῖΟΞμος (nomos, 'custom' or 'law'), hence 'rules of the house(hold)'. Current _____ models developed out of the broader field of political economy in the late 19th century, owing to a desire to use an empirical approach more akin to the physical sciences.
   a. Economic
   b. ACNielsen
   c. Industrial organization
   d. ADTECH

3. The Oxford University Press defines _____ as 'marketing on a worldwide scale reconciling or taking commercial advantage of global operational differences, similarities and opportunities in order to meet global objectives.' Oxford University Press' Glossary of Marketing Terms.

Here are three reasons for the shift from domestic to _____ as given by the authors of the textbook, _____ Management--3rd Edition by Masaaki Kotabe and Kristiaan Helsen, 2004.

One of the product categories in which global competition has been easy to track is in U.S. automotive sales.

   a. Digital marketing
   b. Global marketing
   c. Guerrilla Marketing
   d. Diversity marketing

Chapter 4. The Economic Environment   13

4. _____ is a term used in Internet marketing to define a popular pricing model whereby a marketing agency will receive a bounty from an advertiser for each new lead or new customer obtained for the advertiser through the agency's online marketing efforts. The agency creates advertising campaigns and promotions to convert the maximum number of new leads or customers and gets paid for its work only when a new lead or a new customer is passed on to the advertiser.

PPP advertising became popular with the advent of the world wide web that allows real time measurement of an advertising campaign's ROI (return on investment.)

 a. Power III
 b. 180SearchAssistant
 c. 6-3-5 Brainwriting
 d. Pay for performance advertising

5. _____ is defined by the American _____ Association as the activity, set of institutions, and processes for creating, communicating, delivering, and exchanging offerings that have value for customers, clients, partners, and society at large. The term developed from the original meaning which referred literally to going to market, as in shopping, or going to a market to sell goods or services.

_____ practice tends to be seen as a creative industry, which includes advertising, distribution and selling.

 a. Customer acquisition management
 b. Marketing
 c. Marketing myopia
 d. Product naming

6. A _____ is the space, actual or metaphorical, in which a market operates. The term is also used in a trademark law context to denote the actual consumer environment, ie. the 'real world' in which products and services are provided and consumed.
 a. 6-3-5 Brainwriting
 b. 180SearchAssistant
 c. Marketplace
 d. Power III

7. The _____ or gross domestic income (GDI) is one of the measures of national income and output for a given country's economy. It is the total value of all final goods and services produced in a particular economy; the dollar value of all goods and services produced within a country's borders in a given year. _____ can be defined in three ways, all of which are conceptually identical.

Chapter 4. The Economic Environment

a. Microeconomics
b. Leading indicator
c. Macroeconomics
d. Gross domestic product

8. The United States _____ is the government agency that is responsible for the United States Census. It also gathers other national demographic and economic data.
   a. 180SearchAssistant
   b. Power III
   c. Census Bureau
   d. 6-3-5 Brainwriting

9. A consumer price index (_____) is a measure of the average price of consumer goods and services purchased by households. It is a price index determined by measuring the price of a standard group of goods meant to represent the typical market basket of a typical urban consumer. Related, but different, terms are the _____, the RPI, and the RPIX used in the United Kingdom.
   a. 180SearchAssistant
   b. Power III
   c. Consumer Price Index
   d. CPI

10. _____ is a mathematical science pertaining to the collection, analysis, interpretation or explanation, and presentation of data. It also provides tools for prediction and forecasting based on data. It is applicable to a wide variety of academic disciplines, from the natural and social sciences to the humanities, government and business.
    a. Type I error
    b. Median
    c. Null hypothesis
    d. Statistics

11. _____ is the physical growth of urban areas from rural areas as a result of population immigration to an existing urban area. Effects include change in density and administration services. While the exact definition and population size of urbanized areas varies among different countries, _____ is attributed to growth of cities.
    a. Urbanization
    b. AMAX
    c. ACNielsen
    d. ADTECH

Chapter 4. The Economic Environment

12. _____ refer to a collection of facts usually collected as the result of experience, observation or experiment or a set of premises. This may consist of numbers, words particularly as measurements or observations of a set of variables. _____ are often viewed as a lowest level of abstraction from which information and knowledge are derived.
   a. Pearson product-moment correlation coefficient
   b. Data
   c. Sample size
   d. Mean

13. _____ is a broad label that refers to any individuals or households that use goods and services generated within the economy. The concept of a _____ is used in different contexts, so that the usage and significance of the term may vary.

    A _____ is a person who uses any product or service.

   a. Power III
   b. Consumer
   c. 180SearchAssistant
   d. 6-3-5 Brainwriting

14. _____ or consumer demand or consumption is also known as personal consumption expenditure. It is the largest part of aggregate demand or effective demand at the macroeconomic level. There are two variants of consumption in the aggregate demand model, including induced consumption and autonomous consumption.
   a. Consumer spending
   b. Power III
   c. Deregulation
   d. Value added

15. In economics, _____ is a rise in the general level of prices of goods and services in an economy over a period of time. The term '_____' once referred to increases in the money supply (monetary _____); however, economic debates about the relationship between money supply and price levels have led to its primary use today in describing price _____. Inflation can also be described as a decline in the real value of money--a loss of purchasing power in the medium of exchange which is also the monetary unit of account.
   a. ACNielsen
   b. ADTECH
   c. Industrial organization
   d. Inflation

Chapter 4. The Economic Environment

16. _____ is a form of communication that typically attempts to persuade potential customers to purchase or to consume more of a particular brand of product or service. 'While now central to the contemporary global economy and the reproduction of global production networks, it is only quite recently that _____ has been more than a marginal influence on patterns of sales and production. The formation of modern _____ was intimately bound up with the emergence of new forms of monopoly capitalism around the end of the 19th and beginning of the 20th century as one element in corporate strategies to create, organize and where possible control markets, especially for mass produced consumer goods.

   a. AMAX
   b. ADTECH
   c. Advertising
   d. ACNielsen

17. _____ is a magazine, delivering news, analysis and data on marketing and media. The magazine was started as a broadsheet newspaper in Chicago in 1930. Today, its content appears in a print weekly distributed around the world and on many electronic platforms, including: AdAge.com, daily e-mail newsletters called Ad Age Daily, Ad Age's Mediaworks and Ad Age Digital; weekly newsletters such as Madison ' Vine (about branded entertainment) and Ad Age China; podcasts called Why It Matters and various videos.

   a. Adweek
   b. Ethical Consumer
   c. Outsert
   d. Advertising Age

18. A _____ is a collection of symbols, experiences and associations connected with a product, a service, a person or any other artifact or entity.

   _____s have become increasingly important components of culture and the economy, now being described as 'cultural accessories and personal philosophies'.

   Some people distinguish the psychological aspect of a _____ from the experiential aspect.

   a. Brand
   b. Store brand
   c. Brand equity
   d. Brandable software

19. _____ is a term used to describe how different aspects between economies are integrated. The basics of this theory were written by the Hungarian Economist Béla Balassa in the 1960s. As _____ increases, the barriers of trade between markets diminishes.

a. ACNielsen
b. Incoterms
c. ADTECH
d. Economic integration

20. _____ is a designated group of countries that have agreed to eliminate tariffs, quotas and preferences on most (if not all) goods and services traded between them. It can be considered the second stage of economic integration. Countries choose this kind of economic integration form if their economical structures are complementary.
   a. Power III
   b. 180SearchAssistant
   c. Free trade area
   d. 6-3-5 Brainwriting

21. A _____ is a customs union with common policies on product regulation, and freedom of movement of the factors of production (capital and labour) and of enterprise. The goal is that the movement of capital, labour, goods, and services between the members is as easy as within them. This is the fourth stage of economic integration.
   a. Monetary union
   b. Customs union
   c. Competitive
   d. Common Market

22. _____ is an authority or agency in a country responsible for collecting and safeguarding _____ duties and for controlling the flow of goods including animals, personal effects and hazardous items in and out of a country. Depending on local legislation and regulations, the import or export of some goods may be restricted or forbidden, and the _____ agency enforces these rules. The _____ agency may be different from the immigration authority, which monitors persons who leave or enter the country, checking for appropriate documentation, apprehending people wanted by international arrest warrants, and impeding the entry of others deemed dangerous to the country.
   a. Madrid system for the international registration of marks
   b. Customs
   c. Specific Performance
   d. Registered trademark symbol

23. A _____ is a free trade area with a common external tariff. The participant countries set up common external trade policy, but in some cases they use different import quotas. Common competition policy is also helpful to avoid competition deficiency.

Chapter 4. The Economic Environment

   a. Safeguard
   b. Customs union
   c. Countervailing duties
   d. Zone pricing

24. A _____ is a wide ranging tax, tariff and _____ that often includes investment guarantees. _____s are frequently politically contentious since they may change economic customs and deepen interdependence with trade partners. Increasing efficiency through 'free trade' is a common goal.
   a. Power III
   b. Trade pact
   c. General Agreement on Trade in Services
   d. General Agreement on Tariffs and Trade

25. _____ is the practice of influencing decisions made by government. It includes all attempts to influence legislators and officials, whether by other legislators, constituents or organized groups. A lobbyist is a person who tries to influence legislation on behalf of a special interest or a member of a lobby.
   a. African Americans
   b. AStore
   c. Albert Einstein
   d. Lobbying

26. _____ in organizations and public policy is both the organizational process of creating and maintaining a plan; and the psychological process of thinking about the activities required to create a desired goal on some scale. As such, it is a fundamental property of intelligent behavior. This thought process is essential to the creation and refinement of a plan, or integration of it with other plans, that is, it combines forecasting of developments with the preparation of scenarios of how to react to them.
   a. 6-3-5 Brainwriting
   b. Planning
   c. Power III
   d. 180SearchAssistant

27. _____ is an organization's process of defining its strategy and making decisions on allocating its resources to pursue this strategy, including its capital and people. Various business analysis techniques can be used in _____, including SWOT analysis (Strengths, Weaknesses, Opportunities, and Threats) and PEST analysis (Political, Economic, Social, and Technological analysis) or STEER analysis involving Socio-cultural, Technological, Economic, Ecological, and Regulatory factors and EPISTEL (Environment, Political, Informatic, Social, Technological, Economic and Legal)

Chapter 4. The Economic Environment

_____ is the formal consideration of an organization's future course. All _____ deals with at least one of three key questions:

1. 'What do we do?'
2. 'For whom do we do it?'
3. 'How do we excel?'

In business _____, the third question is better phrased 'How can we beat or avoid competition?'. (Bradford and Duncan, page 1.)

  a. Strategic planning
  b. 6-3-5 Brainwriting
  c. Power III
  d. 180SearchAssistant

28. The term _____ is used to describe a nation's social or business activity in the process of rapid growth and industrialization. Currently, there are approximately 28 _____ in the world, with the economies of China and India considered to be two of the largest. According to The Economist many people find the term dated, but a new term has yet to gain much traction.
  a. ACNielsen
  b. Outsourcing
  c. In-house
  d. Emerging markets

29. Human beings are also considered to be _____ because they have the ability to change raw materials into valuable _____. The term Human _____ can also be defined as the skills, energies, talents, abilities and knowledge that are used for the production of goods or the rendering of services. While taking into account human beings as _____, the following things have to be kept in mind:

- The size of the population
- The capabilities of the individuals in that population

Many _____ cannot be consumed in their original form. They have to be processed in order to change them into more usable commodities.

a. 6-3-5 Brainwriting
b. Resources
c. 180SearchAssistant
d. Power III

Chapter 5. The Political and Legal Environment

1. The Oxford University Press defines _____ as 'marketing on a worldwide scale reconciling or taking commercial advantage of global operational differences, similarities and opportunities in order to meet global objectives.' Oxford University Press' Glossary of Marketing Terms.

Here are three reasons for the shift from domestic to _____ as given by the authors of the textbook, _____ Management--3rd Edition by Masaaki Kotabe and Kristiaan Helsen, 2004.

One of the product categories in which global competition has been easy to track is in U.S. automotive sales.

   a. Diversity marketing
   b. Digital marketing
   c. Guerrilla Marketing
   d. Global marketing

2. _____ is defined by the American _____ Association as the activity, set of institutions, and processes for creating, communicating, delivering, and exchanging offerings that have value for customers, clients, partners, and society at large. The term developed from the original meaning which referred literally to going to market, as in shopping, or going to a market to sell goods or services.

   _____ practice tends to be seen as a creative industry, which includes advertising, distribution and selling.

   a. Customer acquisition management
   b. Marketing myopia
   c. Product naming
   d. Marketing

3. In economics, an _____ is any good or commodity, transported from one country to another country in a legitimate fashion, typically for use in trade. _____ goods or services are provided to foreign consumers by domestic producers. _____ is an important part of international trade.
   a. ADTECH
   b. ACNielsen
   c. Export
   d. AMAX

4. A _____ is a tax imposed on goods when they are moved across a political boundary. They are usually associated with protectionism, the economic policy of restraining trade between nations. For political reasons, _____s are usually imposed on imported goods, although they may also be imposed on exported goods.

Chapter 5. The Political and Legal Environment

a. Power III
b. Monetary policy
c. Tariff
d. Fiscal policy

5. _____ refers to 'controlling human or societal behaviour by rules or restrictions.' _____ can take many forms: legal restrictions promulgated by a government authority, self-_____, social _____, co-_____ and market _____. One can consider _____ as actions of conduct imposing sanctions (such as a fine.) This action of administrative law, or implementing regulatory law, may be contrasted with statutory or case law.
   a. Regulation
   b. Rule of four
   c. Non-conventional trademark
   d. CAN-SPAM

6. _____ is the state or fact of exclusive rights and control over property, which may be an object, land/real estate, or some other kind of property (like government-granted monopolies collectively referred to as intellectual property.) It is embodied in an _____ right also referred to as title.

   _____ is the key building block in the development of the capitalist socio-economic system.

   a. AMAX
   b. ACNielsen
   c. ADTECH
   d. Ownership

7. _____ is a concept that denotes the precise probability of specific eventualities. Technically, the notion of _____ is independent from the notion of value and, as such, eventualities may have both beneficial and adverse consequences. However, in general usage the convention is to focus only on potential negative impact to some characteristic of value that may arise from a future event.
   a. Risk
   b. Power III
   c. 6-3-5 Brainwriting
   d. 180SearchAssistant

8. _____ is a technique used in propaganda and advertising. Also known as association, this is a technique of projecting positive or negative qualities (praise or blame) of a person, entity, object, or value (an individual, group, organization, nation, patriotism, etc.) to another in order to make the second more acceptable or to discredit it.

a. Transfer
b. Sexism,
c. Micro ads
d. Supplier

9. _____ in economics and business is the result of an exchange and from that trade we assign a numerical monetary value to a good, service or asset. If I trade 4 apples for an orange, the _____ of an orange is 4 - apples. Inversely, the _____ of an apple is 1/4 oranges.
a. Contribution margin-based pricing
b. Discounts and allowances
c. Pricing
d. Price

10. _____ is a branch of philosophy which seeks to address questions about morality, such as how a moral outcome can be achieved in a specific situation (applied _____), how moral values should be determined (normative _____), what moral values people actually abide by (descriptive _____), what the fundamental semantic, ontological, and epistemic nature of _____ or morality is (meta-_____), and how moral capacity or moral agency develops and what its nature is (moral psychology.)

Socrates was one of the first Greek philosophers to encourage both scholars and the common citizen to turn their attention from the outside world to the condition of man. In this view, Knowledge having a bearing on human life was placed highest, all other knowledge being secondary.

a. AMAX
b. ADTECH
c. ACNielsen
d. Ethics

11. In psychology, philosophy, and the cognitive sciences, _____ is the process of attaining awareness or understanding of sensory information. It is a task far more complex than was imagined in the 1950s and 1960s, when it was predicted that building perceiving machines would take about a decade, a goal which is still very far from fruition. The word _____ comes from the Latin words _____, percepio, meaning 'receiving, collecting, action of taking possession, apprehension with the mind or senses.'

_____ is one of the oldest fields in psychology.

Chapter 5. The Political and Legal Environment

   a. Power III
   b. 180SearchAssistant
   c. Groupthink
   d. Perception

12. _____s is the social science that studies the production, distribution, and consumption of goods and services. The term _____s comes from the Ancient Greek oá¼°κονομῖα from oá¼¶κος (oikos, 'house') + vÏŒμος (nomos, 'custom' or 'law'), hence 'rules of the house(hold)'. Current _____ models developed out of the broader field of political economy in the late 19th century, owing to a desire to use an empirical approach more akin to the physical sciences.
   a. ACNielsen
   b. Economic
   c. ADTECH
   d. Industrial organization

13. _____ is an authority or agency in a country responsible for collecting and safeguarding _____ duties and for controlling the flow of goods including animals, personal effects and hazardous items in and out of a country. Depending on local legislation and regulations, the import or export of some goods may be restricted or forbidden, and the _____ agency enforces these rules. The _____ agency may be different from the immigration authority, which monitors persons who leave or enter the country, checking for appropriate documentation, apprehending people wanted by international arrest warrants, and impeding the entry of others deemed dangerous to the country.
   a. Customs
   b. Madrid system for the international registration of marks
   c. Registered trademark symbol
   d. Specific Performance

14. _____ is exchange of capital, goods, and services across international borders or territories. In most countries, it represents a significant share of gross domestic product (GDP.) While _____ has been present throughout much of history , its economic, social, and political importance has been on the rise in recent centuries.
   a. Incoterms
   b. ACNielsen
   c. ADTECH
   d. International Trade

15. _____ is an advertisement in which a particular product specifically mentions a competitor by name for the express purpose of showing why the competitor is inferior to the product naming it.

This should not be confused with parody advertisements, where a fictional product is being advertised for the purpose of poking fun at the particular advertisement, nor should it be confused with the use of a coined brand name for the purpose of comparing the product without actually naming an actual competitor. ('Wikipedia tastes better and is less filling than the Encyclopedia Galactica.')

In the 1980s, during what has been referred to as the cola wars, soft-drink manufacturer Pepsi ran a series of advertisements where people, caught on hidden camera, in a blind taste test, chose Pepsi over rival Coca-Cola.

   a. GL-70
   b. Cost per conversion
   c. Heavy-up
   d. Comparative advertising

16. The General Agreement on Tariffs and Trade was the outcome of the failure of negotiating governments to create the International Trade Organization (ITO.) _____ was formed in 1947 and lasted until 1994, when it was replaced by the World Trade Organization. The Bretton Woods Conference had introduced the idea for an organization to regulate trade as part of a larger plan for economic recovery after World War II.
   a. Power III
   b. General Agreement on Tariffs and Trade
   c. Trade pact
   d. GATT

Chapter 6. Strategic Planning

1. _____s is the social science that studies the production, distribution, and consumption of goods and services. The term _____s comes from the Ancient Greek oá¼°κονομῖα from oá¼¶κος (oikos, 'house') + vĺŒμος (nomos, 'custom' or 'law'), hence 'rules of the house(hold)'. Current _____ models developed out of the broader field of political economy in the late 19th century, owing to a desire to use an empirical approach more akin to the physical sciences.

   a. Industrial organization
   b. ADTECH
   c. ACNielsen
   d. Economic

2. The Oxford University Press defines _____ as 'marketing on a worldwide scale reconciling or taking commercial advantage of global operational differences, similarities and opportunities in order to meet global objectives.' Oxford University Press' Glossary of Marketing Terms.

   Here are three reasons for the shift from domestic to _____ as given by the authors of the textbook, _____ Management--3rd Edition by Masaaki Kotabe and Kristiaan Helsen, 2004.

   One of the product categories in which global competition has been easy to track is in U.S. automotive sales.

   a. Guerrilla Marketing
   b. Diversity marketing
   c. Global marketing
   d. Digital marketing

3. _____ is defined by the American _____ Association as the activity, set of institutions, and processes for creating, communicating, delivering, and exchanging offerings that have value for customers, clients, partners, and society at large. The term developed from the original meaning which referred literally to going to market, as in shopping, or going to a market to sell goods or services.

   _____ practice tends to be seen as a creative industry, which includes advertising, distribution and selling.

   a. Customer acquisition management
   b. Marketing myopia
   c. Product naming
   d. Marketing

4. _____ in organizations and public policy is both the organizational process of creating and maintaining a plan; and the psychological process of thinking about the activities required to create a desired goal on some scale. As such, it is a fundamental property of intelligent behavior. This thought process is essential to the creation and refinement of a plan, or integration of it with other plans, that is, it combines forecasting of developments with the preparation of scenarios of how to react to them.

a. 180SearchAssistant
b. Power III
c. 6-3-5 Brainwriting
d. Planning

5. _____ is an organization's process of defining its strategy and making decisions on allocating its resources to pursue this strategy, including its capital and people. Various business analysis techniques can be used in _____, including SWOT analysis (Strengths, Weaknesses, Opportunities, and Threats) and PEST analysis (Political, Economic, Social, and Technological analysis) or STEER analysis involving Socio-cultural, Technological, Economic, Ecological, and Regulatory factors and EPISTEL (Environment, Political, Informatic, Social, Technological, Economic and Legal)

_____ is the formal consideration of an organization's future course. All _____ deals with at least one of three key questions:

1. 'What do we do?'
2. 'For whom do we do it?'
3. 'How do we excel?'

In business _____, the third question is better phrased 'How can we beat or avoid competition?'. (Bradford and Duncan, page 1.)

a. 180SearchAssistant
b. Power III
c. 6-3-5 Brainwriting
d. Strategic planning

6. In economics, business, retail, and accounting, a _____ is the value of money that has been used up to produce something, and hence is not available for use anymore. In economics, a _____ is an alternative that is given up as a result of a decision. In business, the _____ may be one of acquisition, in which case the amount of money expended to acquire it is counted as _____.
a. Transaction cost
b. Cost
c. Variable cost
d. Fixed costs

7. _____ in its literal sense is the process of transformation of local or regional phenomena into global ones. It can be described as a process by which the people of the world are unified into a single society and function together.

This process is a combination of economic, technological, sociocultural and political forces.

a. 6-3-5 Brainwriting
b. 180SearchAssistant
c. Power III
d. Globalization

8. Competitiveness is a comparative concept of the ability and performance of a firm, sub-sector or country to sell and supply goods and/or services in a given market. Although widely used in economics and business management, the usefulness of the concept, particularly in the context of national competitiveness, is vigorously disputed by economists, such as Paul Krugman.

The term may also be applied to markets, where it is used to refer to the extent to which the market structure may be regarded as perfectly _____.

a. Customs union
b. Competitive
c. Geographical pricing
d. Free trade zone

9. A _____ is the space, actual or metaphorical, in which a market operates. The term is also used in a trademark law context to denote the actual consumer environment, ie. the 'real world' in which products and services are provided and consumed.
a. Marketplace
b. Power III
c. 6-3-5 Brainwriting
d. 180SearchAssistant

10. A _____ is a tax imposed on goods when they are moved across a political boundary. They are usually associated with protectionism, the economic policy of restraining trade between nations. For political reasons, _____s are usually imposed on imported goods, although they may also be imposed on exported goods.
a. Fiscal policy
b. Power III
c. Monetary policy
d. Tariff

11. Organizational culture is not the same as _____. It is wider and deeper concepts, something that an organization 'is' rather than what it 'has' (according to Buchanan and Huczynski.)

_____ is the total sum of the values, customs, traditions and meanings that make a company unique.

Chapter 6. Strategic Planning

a. Cross-functional team
b. Power III
c. 180SearchAssistant
d. Corporate culture

12. _____ is difficult to define. For example, in 1952, Alfred Kroeber and Clyde Kluckhohn compiled a list of 164 definitions of '_____' in _____: A Critical Review of Concepts and Definitions. However, the word '_____' is most commonly used in three basic senses:

- excellence of taste in the fine arts and humanities
- an integrated pattern of human knowledge, belief, and behavior that depends upon the capacity for symbolic thought and social learning
- the set of shared attitudes, values, goals, and practices that characterizes an institution, organization or group.

When the concept first emerged in eighteenth- and nineteenth-century Europe, it connoted a process of cultivation or improvement, as in agriculture or horticulture. In the nineteenth century, it came to refer first to the betterment or refinement of the individual, especially through education, and then to the fulfillment of national aspirations or ideals.

a. Culture
b. AStore
c. Albert Einstein
d. African Americans

13. The _____ or gross domestic income (GDI) is one of the measures of national income and output for a given country's economy. It is the total value of all final goods and services produced in a particular economy; the dollar value of all goods and services produced within a country's borders in a given year. _____ can be defined in three ways, all of which are conceptually identical.
a. Leading indicator
b. Microeconomics
c. Macroeconomics
d. Gross domestic product

Chapter 7. Marketing Organization, Implementation, and Control

1. _____s is the social science that studies the production, distribution, and consumption of goods and services. The term _____s comes from the Ancient Greek oá¼°κονομῖα from oá¼¶κος (oikos, 'house') + vĺŒµος (nomos, 'custom' or 'law'), hence 'rules of the house(hold)'. Current _____ models developed out of the broader field of political economy in the late 19th century, owing to a desire to use an empirical approach more akin to the physical sciences.
   a. ADTECH
   b. ACNielsen
   c. Industrial organization
   d. Economic

2. The Oxford University Press defines _____ as 'marketing on a worldwide scale reconciling or taking commercial advantage of global operational differences, similarities and opportunities in order to meet global objectives.' Oxford University Press' Glossary of Marketing Terms.

Here are three reasons for the shift from domestic to _____ as given by the authors of the textbook, _____ Management--3rd Edition by Masaaki Kotabe and Kristiaan Helsen, 2004.

One of the product categories in which global competition has been easy to track is in U.S. automotive sales.

   a. Guerrilla Marketing
   b. Digital marketing
   c. Diversity marketing
   d. Global marketing

3. _____ is the realization of an application idea, model, design, specification, standard, algorithm an _____ is a realization of a technical specification or algorithm as a program, software component, or other computer system. Many _____s may exist for a given specification or standard.
   a. AMAX
   b. ADTECH
   c. ACNielsen
   d. Implementation

4. _____ is the management of the flow of goods, information and other resources, including energy and people, between the point of origin and the point of consumption in order to meet the requirements of consumers (frequently, and originally, military organizations.) _____ involves the integration of information, transportation, inventory, warehousing, material-handling, and packaging. _____ is a channel of the supply chain which adds the value of time and place utility.
   a. Power III
   b. 6-3-5 Brainwriting
   c. 180SearchAssistant
   d. Logistics

Chapter 7. Marketing Organization, Implementation, and Control

5. _____ is defined by the American _____ Association as the activity, set of institutions, and processes for creating, communicating, delivering, and exchanging offerings that have value for customers, clients, partners, and society at large. The term developed from the original meaning which referred literally to going to market, as in shopping, or going to a market to sell goods or services.

_____ practice tends to be seen as a creative industry, which includes advertising, distribution and selling.

a. Marketing myopia
b. Product naming
c. Customer acquisition management
d. Marketing

6. _____ is the branch of logistics that deals with the tangible components of a supply chain. Specifically, this covers the acquisition of spare parts and replacements, quality control of purchasing and ordering such parts, and the standards involved in ordering, shipping, and warehousing the said parts.

A large component of _____ is ensuring that parts and materials used in the supply chain meet minimum requirements by performing quality assurance (QA.)

a. Reverse auction
b. Customer driven supply chain
c. Vendor Managed Inventory
d. Materials management

7. _____ is an advertisement in which a particular product specifically mentions a competitor by name for the express purpose of showing why the competitor is inferior to the product naming it.

This should not be confused with parody advertisements, where a fictional product is being advertised for the purpose of poking fun at the particular advertisement, nor should it be confused with the use of a coined brand name for the purpose of comparing the product without actually naming an actual competitor. ('Wikipedia tastes better and is less filling than the Encyclopedia Galactica.')

In the 1980s, during what has been referred to as the cola wars, soft-drink manufacturer Pepsi ran a series of advertisements where people, caught on hidden camera, in a blind taste test, chose Pepsi over rival Coca-Cola.

a. GL-70
b. Cost per conversion
c. Heavy-up
d. Comparative advertising

Chapter 7. Marketing Organization, Implementation, and Control

8. _____ measures the performance of a system. Certain goals are defined and the _____ gives the percentage to which they should be achieved.

Examples

- Percentage of calls answered in a call center.
- Percentage of customers waiting less than a given fixed time.
- Percentage of customers that do not experience a stock out.

_____ is used in supply chain management and in inventory management to measure the performance of inventory systems.

Under stochastic conditions it is unavoidable that in some periods the inventory on hand is not sufficient to deliver the complete demand and, as a consequence, that part of the demand is filled only after an inventory-related waiting time.

 a. Nielsen SoundScan
 b. False designation of origin
 c. Symbol group
 d. Service level

9. A _____ is a customs union with common policies on product regulation, and freedom of movement of the factors of production (capital and labour) and of enterprise. The goal is that the movement of capital, labour, goods, and services between the members is as easy as within them. This is the fourth stage of economic integration.
 a. Competitive
 b. Monetary union
 c. Customs union
 d. Common Market

10. _____ involves disseminating information about a product, product line, brand, or company. It is one of the four key aspects of the marketing mix. (The other three elements are product marketing, pricing, and distribution). P>_____ is generally sub-divided into two parts:

- Above the line _____: Promotion in the media (e.g. TV, radio, newspapers, Internet and Mobile Phones) in which the advertiser pays an advertising agency to place the ad
- Below the line _____: All other _____. Much of this is intended to be subtle enough for the consumer to be unaware that _____ is taking place. E.g. sponsorship, product placement, endorsements, sales _____, merchandising, direct mail, personal selling, public relations, trade shows

a. Bottling lines
b. Cashmere Agency
c. Davie Brown Index
d. Promotion

Chapter 8. Research

1. _____s is the social science that studies the production, distribution, and consumption of goods and services. The term _____s comes from the Ancient Greek oá¼°κονομῑα from oá¼¶κος (oikos, 'house') + vÍŒμος (nomos, 'custom' or 'law'), hence 'rules of the house(hold)'. Current _____ models developed out of the broader field of political economy in the late 19th century, owing to a desire to use an empirical approach more akin to the physical sciences.

   a. Economic
   b. Industrial organization
   c. ADTECH
   d. ACNielsen

2. The Oxford University Press defines _____ as 'marketing on a worldwide scale reconciling or taking commercial advantage of global operational differences, similarities and opportunities in order to meet global objectives.' Oxford University Press' Glossary of Marketing Terms.

   Here are three reasons for the shift from domestic to _____ as given by the authors of the textbook, _____ Management--3rd Edition by Masaaki Kotabe and Kristiaan Helsen, 2004.

   One of the product categories in which global competition has been easy to track is in U.S. automotive sales.

   a. Guerrilla Marketing
   b. Diversity marketing
   c. Digital marketing
   d. Global marketing

3. _____ is defined by the American _____ Association as the activity, set of institutions, and processes for creating, communicating, delivering, and exchanging offerings that have value for customers, clients, partners, and society at large. The term developed from the original meaning which referred literally to going to market, as in shopping, or going to a market to sell goods or services.

   _____ practice tends to be seen as a creative industry, which includes advertising, distribution and selling.

   a. Marketing
   b. Customer acquisition management
   c. Product naming
   d. Marketing myopia

4. _____ is exchange of capital, goods, and services across international borders or territories. In most countries, it represents a significant share of gross domestic product (GDP.) While _____ has been present throughout much of history, its economic, social, and political importance has been on the rise in recent centuries.

Chapter 8. Research 35

a. ACNielsen
b. ADTECH
c. Incoterms
d. International Trade

5. _____ is an advertisement in which a particular product specifically mentions a competitor by name for the express purpose of showing why the competitor is inferior to the product naming it.

This should not be confused with parody advertisements, where a fictional product is being advertised for the purpose of poking fun at the particular advertisement, nor should it be confused with the use of a coined brand name for the purpose of comparing the product without actually naming an actual competitor. ('Wikipedia tastes better and is less filling than the Encyclopedia Galactica.')

In the 1980s, during what has been referred to as the cola wars, soft-drink manufacturer Pepsi ran a series of advertisements where people, caught on hidden camera, in a blind taste test, chose Pepsi over rival Coca-Cola.

a. Heavy-up
b. Cost per conversion
c. Comparative advertising
d. GL-70

6. _____ refer to a collection of facts usually collected as the result of experience, observation or experiment or a set of premises. This may consist of numbers, words particularly as measurements or observations of a set of variables. _____ are often viewed as a lowest level of abstraction from which information and knowledge are derived.

a. Data
b. Sample size
c. Mean
d. Pearson product-moment correlation coefficient

7. _____ is systematic determination of merit, worth, and significance of something or someone using criteria against a set of standards. _____ often is used to characterize and appraise subjects of interest in a wide range of human enterprises, including the arts, criminal justice, foundations and non-profit organizations, government, health care, and other human services.

Depending on the topic of interest, there are professional groups which look to the quality and rigor of the _____ process.

a. AMAX
b. ADTECH
c. ACNielsen
d. Evaluation

8. _____ is a broad label that refers to any individuals or households that use goods and services generated within the economy. The concept of a _____ is used in different contexts, so that the usage and significance of the term may vary.

A _____ is a person who uses any product or service.

a. 180SearchAssistant
b. Power III
c. 6-3-5 Brainwriting
d. Consumer

9. _____ is a radio audience research company in the United States which collects listener data on radio audiences similar to that collected by Nielsen Media Research on television audiences. It was founded as American Research Bureau by Jim Seiler in 1949 and became bi-coastal by merging with L.A. based Coffin, Cooper and Clay in the early 1950s. ARB's initial business was the collection of television broadcast ratings exclusively.

a. American Heart Association
b. Access Commerce
c. American Cancer Society
d. Arbitron

10. In economics, an externality or spillover of an economic transaction is an impact on a party that is not directly involved in the transaction. In such a case, prices do not reflect the full costs or benefits in production or consumption of a product or service. A positive impact is called an _____ benefit, while a negative impact is called an _____ cost.

a. ADTECH
b. External
c. ACNielsen
d. AMAX

Chapter 8. Research

11. Human beings are also considered to be _____ because they have the ability to change raw materials into valuable _____. The term Human _____ can also be defined as the skills, energies, talents, abilities and knowledge that are used for the production of goods or the rendering of services. While taking into account human beings as _____, the following things have to be kept in mind:

- The size of the population
- The capabilities of the individuals in that population

Many _____ cannot be consumed in their original form. They have to be processed in order to change them into more usable commodities.

   a. 180SearchAssistant
   b. Power III
   c. 6-3-5 Brainwriting
   d. Resources

12. A _____ is a form of qualitative research in which a group of people are asked about their attitude towards a product, service, concept, advertisement, idea, or packaging. Questions are asked in an interactive group setting where participants are free to talk with other group members.

Ernest Dichter originated the idea of having a 'group therapy' for products and this process is what became known as a _____.

   a. Marketing research process
   b. Cross tabulation
   c. Logit analysis
   d. Focus group

13. A _____ is a relatively new executive level position at a corporation, company, organization typically reporting directly to the CEO or board of directors. The _____ is responsible for a brand's image, experience, and promise, and propagating it throughout all aspects of the company. The brand officer oversees marketing, advertising, design, public relations and customer service departments.
   a. Power III
   b. Chief executive officer
   c. Financial analyst
   d. Chief brand officer

14. _____ is a term used to describe how different aspects between economies are integrated. The basics of this theory were written by the Hungarian Economist Béla Balassa in the 1960s. As _____ increases, the barriers of trade between markets diminishes.

a. ADTECH
b. ACNielsen
c. Incoterms
d. Economic integration

15. The United States _____ is the government agency that is responsible for the United States Census. It also gathers other national demographic and economic data.
   a. Power III
   b. Census Bureau
   c. 6-3-5 Brainwriting
   d. 180SearchAssistant

16. _____ is an authority or agency in a country responsible for collecting and safeguarding _____ duties and for controlling the flow of goods including animals, personal effects and hazardous items in and out of a country. Depending on local legislation and regulations, the import or export of some goods may be restricted or forbidden, and the _____ agency enforces these rules. The _____ agency may be different from the immigration authority, which monitors persons who leave or enter the country, checking for appropriate documentation, apprehending people wanted by international arrest warrants, and impeding the entry of others deemed dangerous to the country.
   a. Madrid system for the international registration of marks
   b. Registered trademark symbol
   c. Specific Performance
   d. Customs

17. _____, commonly known as e-commerce or eCommerce, consists of the buying and selling of products or services over electronic systems such as the Internet and other computer networks. The amount of trade conducted electronically has grown extraordinarily with wide-spread Internet usage. A wide variety of commerce is conducted in this way, spurring and drawing on innovations in electronic funds transfer, supply chain management, Internet marketing, online transaction processing, electronic data interchange (EDI), inventory management systems, and automated data collection systems.
   a. ACNielsen
   b. AMAX
   c. Electronic commerce
   d. ADTECH

Chapter 8. Research 39

18. _____ is a form of communication that typically attempts to persuade potential customers to purchase or to consume more of a particular brand of product or service. 'While now central to the contemporary global economy and the reproduction of global production networks, it is only quite recently that _____ has been more than a marginal influence on patterns of sales and production. The formation of modern _____ was intimately bound up with the emergence of new forms of monopoly capitalism around the end of the 19th and beginning of the 20th century as one element in corporate strategies to create, organize and where possible control markets, especially for mass produced consumer goods.
   a. ACNielsen
   b. Advertising
   c. AMAX
   d. ADTECH

19. _____ is a magazine, delivering news, analysis and data on marketing and media. The magazine was started as a broadsheet newspaper in Chicago in 1930. Today, its content appears in a print weekly distributed around the world and on many electronic platforms, including: AdAge.com, daily e-mail newsletters called Ad Age Daily, Ad Age's Mediaworks and Ad Age Digital; weekly newsletters such as Madison ' Vine (about branded entertainment) and Ad Age China; podcasts called Why It Matters and various videos.
   a. Outsert
   b. Ethical Consumer
   c. Adweek
   d. Advertising Age

20. The _____ is a professional association for marketers. As of 2008 it had approximately 40,000 members. There are collegiate chapters on 250 campuses.
   a. ADTECH
   b. ACNielsen
   c. American Marketing Association
   d. AMAX

21. In economics, an _____ is any good or commodity, transported from one country to another country in a legitimate fashion, typically for use in trade. _____ goods or services are provided to foreign consumers by domestic producers. _____ is an important part of international trade.
   a. ADTECH
   b. ACNielsen
   c. AMAX
   d. Export

Chapter 8. Research

22. _____ is a measure of the strength of a brand, product, service relative to competitive offerings. There is often a geographic element to the competitive landscape. In defining _____, you must see to what extent a product, brand, or firm controls a product category in a given geographic area.
    a. Market system
    b. Discretionary spending
    c. Productivity
    d. Market dominance

23. _____ is a mathematical science pertaining to the collection, analysis, interpretation or explanation, and presentation of data. It also provides tools for prediction and forecasting based on data. It is applicable to a wide variety of academic disciplines, from the natural and social sciences to the humanities, government and business.
    a. Type I error
    b. Statistics
    c. Median
    d. Null hypothesis

24. The _____ is an international financial institution that provides financial and technical assistance to developing countries for development programs (e.g. bridges, roads, schools, etc.) with the stated goal of reducing poverty.

The _____ differs from the _____ Group, in that the _____ comprises only two institutions:

- International Bank for Reconstruction and Development (IBRD)
- International Development Association (IDA)

Whereas the latter incorporates these two in addition to three more:

- International Finance Corporation (IFC)
- Multilateral Investment Guarantee Agency (MIGA)
- International Centre for Settlement of Investment Disputes (ICSID)

John Maynard Keynes (right) represented the UK at the conference, and Harry Dexter White represented the US.

The _____ was created following the ratification of the United Nations Monetary and Financial Conference of the Bretton Woods agreement. The concept was originally conceived in July 1944 at the United Nations Monetary and Financial Conference.

a. 180SearchAssistant
b. World Bank
c. 6-3-5 Brainwriting
d. Power III

Chapter 9. Market Entry and Expansion

1. _____s is the social science that studies the production, distribution, and consumption of goods and services. The term _____s comes from the Ancient Greek oá¼°κονομῖα from oá¼¶κος (oikos, 'house') + vΐŒμος (nomos, 'custom' or 'law'), hence 'rules of the house(hold)'. Current _____ models developed out of the broader field of political economy in the late 19th century, owing to a desire to use an empirical approach more akin to the physical sciences.
    a. Economic
    b. ACNielsen
    c. ADTECH
    d. Industrial organization

2. The Oxford University Press defines _____ as 'marketing on a worldwide scale reconciling or taking commercial advantage of global operational differences, similarities and opportunities in order to meet global objectives.' Oxford University Press' Glossary of Marketing Terms.

Here are three reasons for the shift from domestic to _____ as given by the authors of the textbook, _____ Management--3rd Edition by Masaaki Kotabe and Kristiaan Helsen, 2004.

One of the product categories in which global competition has been easy to track is in U.S. automotive sales.

   a. Diversity marketing
   b. Guerrilla Marketing
   c. Digital marketing
   d. Global marketing

3. _____ is defined by the American _____ Association as the activity, set of institutions, and processes for creating, communicating, delivering, and exchanging offerings that have value for customers, clients, partners, and society at large. The term developed from the original meaning which referred literally to going to market, as in shopping, or going to a market to sell goods or services.

_____ practice tends to be seen as a creative industry, which includes advertising, distribution and selling.

   a. Marketing myopia
   b. Marketing
   c. Customer acquisition management
   d. Product naming

4. A _____ is the space, actual or metaphorical, in which a market operates. The term is also used in a trademark law context to denote the actual consumer environment, ie. the 'real world' in which products and services are provided and consumed.

a. Power III
b. 180SearchAssistant
c. 6-3-5 Brainwriting
d. Marketplace

5. _____ is exchange of capital, goods, and services across international borders or territories. In most countries, it represents a significant share of gross domestic product (GDP.) While _____ has been present throughout much of history , its economic, social, and political importance has been on the rise in recent centuries.
a. Incoterms
b. International Trade
c. ACNielsen
d. ADTECH

6. A _____ is a relatively new executive level position at a corporation, company, organization typically reporting directly to the CEO or board of directors. The _____ is responsible for a brand's image, experience, and promise, and propagating it throughout all aspects of the company. The brand officer oversees marketing, advertising, design, public relations and customer service departments.
a. Chief brand officer
b. Financial analyst
c. Power III
d. Chief executive officer

7. In economics, an _____ is any good or commodity, transported from one country to another country in a legitimate fashion, typically for use in trade. _____ goods or services are provided to foreign consumers by domestic producers. _____ is an important part of international trade.
a. ADTECH
b. ACNielsen
c. Export
d. AMAX

8. In economics, an externality or spillover of an economic transaction is an impact on a party that is not directly involved in the transaction. In such a case, prices do not reflect the full costs or benefits in production or consumption of a product or service. A positive impact is called an _____ benefit, while a negative impact is called an _____ cost.

Chapter 9. Market Entry and Expansion

a. ACNielsen
b. External
c. AMAX
d. ADTECH

9. Electronic commerce, commonly known as _____ or eCommerce, consists of the buying and selling of products or services over electronic systems such as the Internet and other computer networks. The amount of trade conducted electronically has grown extraordinarily with wide-spread Internet usage. A wide variety of commerce is conducted in this way, spurring and drawing on innovations in electronic funds transfer, supply chain management, Internet marketing, online transaction processing, electronic data interchange (EDI), inventory management systems, and automated data collection systems.

a. E-commerce
b. ACNielsen
c. AMAX
d. ADTECH

10. _____ refers to the methods of practicing and using another person's philosophy of business. The franchisor grants the independent operator the right to distribute its products, techniques, and trademarks for a percentage of gross monthly sales and a royalty fee. Various tangibles and intangibles such as national or international advertising, training, and other support services are commonly made available by the franchisor.

a. 180SearchAssistant
b. Power III
c. Franchise fee
d. Franchising

11. _____ is the practice of managing the flow of information between an organization and its publics. _____ - often referred to as _____ - gains an organization or individual exposure to their audiences using topics of public interest and news items that do not require direct payment. Because _____ places exposure in credible third-party outlets, it offers a third-party legitimacy that advertising does not have.

a. Graphic communication
b. Symbolic analysis
c. Power III
d. Public relations

12. _____ is an advertisement in which a particular product specifically mentions a competitor by name for the express purpose of showing why the competitor is inferior to the product naming it.

Chapter 9. Market Entry and Expansion

This should not be confused with parody advertisements, where a fictional product is being advertised for the purpose of poking fun at the particular advertisement, nor should it be confused with the use of a coined brand name for the purpose of comparing the product without actually naming an actual competitor. ('Wikipedia tastes better and is less filling than the Encyclopedia Galactica.')

In the 1980s, during what has been referred to as the cola wars, soft-drink manufacturer Pepsi ran a series of advertisements where people, caught on hidden camera, in a blind taste test, chose Pepsi over rival Coca-Cola.

   a. Cost per conversion
   b. GL-70
   c. Heavy-up
   d. Comparative advertising

13.   The verb _____ or grant _____ means to give permission. The noun _____ refers to that permission as well as to the document memorializing that permission. _____ may be granted by a party to another party as an element of an agreement between those parties.
   a. 6-3-5 Brainwriting
   b. 180SearchAssistant
   c. Power III
   d. License

14.   _____ is an inventory strategy implemented to improve the return on investment of a business by reducing in-process inventory and its associated carrying costs. In order to achieve JIT the process must have signals of what is going on elsewhere within the process. This means that the process is often driven by a series of signals, which can be Kanban , that tell production processes when to make the next part.
   a. Promotion
   b. Clutter
   c. Personalization
   d. Just-in-time

15.   In economics and sociology, an _____ is any factor (financial or non-financial) that enables or motivates a particular course of action, or counts as a reason for preferring one choice to the alternatives. It is an expectation that encourages people to behave in a certain way. Since human beings are purposeful creatures, the study of _____ structures is central to the study of all economic activity (both in terms of individual decision-making and in terms of co-operation and competition within a larger institutional structure.)

a. ADTECH
b. ACNielsen
c. Incentive
d. AMAX

16. A _____ is an entity formed between two or more parties to undertake economic activity together. The parties agree to create a new entity by both contributing equity, and they then share in the revenues, expenses, and control of the enterprise. The venture can be for one specific project only, or a continuing business relationship such as the Fuji Xerox _____.

a. Consumer protection
b. Gripe site
c. Joint venture
d. Trademark attorney

17. _____ is the state or fact of exclusive rights and control over property, which may be an object, land/real estate, or some other kind of property (like government-granted monopolies collectively referred to as intellectual property.) It is embodied in an _____ right also referred to as title.

_____ is the key building block in the development of the capitalist socio-economic system.

a. Ownership
b. AMAX
c. ACNielsen
d. ADTECH

18. Human beings are also considered to be _____ because they have the ability to change raw materials into valuable _____. The term Human _____ can also be defined as the skills, energies, talents, abilities and knowledge that are used for the production of goods or the rendering of services. While taking into account human beings as _____, the following things have to be kept in mind:

- The size of the population
- The capabilities of the individuals in that population

Many _____ cannot be consumed in their original form. They have to be processed in order to change them into more usable commodities.

a. 6-3-5 Brainwriting
b. Power III
c. Resources
d. 180SearchAssistant

Chapter 10. Product Adaptation

1. In economics, an _____ is any good or commodity, transported from one country to another country in a legitimate fashion, typically for use in trade. _____ goods or services are provided to foreign consumers by domestic producers. _____ is an important part of international trade.
   a. AMAX
   b. ACNielsen
   c. Export
   d. ADTECH

2. The Oxford University Press defines _____ as 'marketing on a worldwide scale reconciling or taking commercial advantage of global operational differences, similarities and opportunities in order to meet global objectives.' Oxford University Press' Glossary of Marketing Terms.

   Here are three reasons for the shift from domestic to _____ as given by the authors of the textbook, _____ Management--3rd Edition by Masaaki Kotabe and Kristiaan Helsen, 2004.

   One of the product categories in which global competition has been easy to track is in U.S. automotive sales.

   a. Digital marketing
   b. Diversity marketing
   c. Guerrilla Marketing
   d. Global marketing

3. _____ is defined by the American _____ Association as the activity, set of institutions, and processes for creating, communicating, delivering, and exchanging offerings that have value for customers, clients, partners, and society at large. The term developed from the original meaning which referred literally to going to market, as in shopping, or going to a market to sell goods or services.

   _____ practice tends to be seen as a creative industry, which includes advertising, distribution and selling.

   a. Marketing
   b. Customer acquisition management
   c. Product naming
   d. Marketing myopia

4. A _____ is the space, actual or metaphorical, in which a market operates. The term is also used in a trademark law context to denote the actual consumer environment, ie. the 'real world' in which products and services are provided and consumed.

Chapter 10. Product Adaptation

a. Marketplace
b. 6-3-5 Brainwriting
c. Power III
d. 180SearchAssistant

5. _____s are used in open sentences. For instance, in the formula x + 1 = 5, x is a _____ which represents an 'unknown' number. _____s are often represented by letters of the Roman alphabet, or those of other alphabets, such as Greek, and use other special symbols.

a. Book of business
b. Quantitative
c. Variable
d. Personalization

6. The _____ is a marketing term and refers to all of the forces outside of marketing that affect marketing management's ability to build and maintain successful relationships with target customers. The _____ consists of both the macroenvironment and the microenvironment.

The microenvironment refers to the forces that are close to the company and affect its ability to serve its customers.

a. Psychographic
b. Market Environment
c. Business-to-consumer
d. Customer franchise

7. _____ refers to 'controlling human or societal behaviour by rules or restrictions.' _____ can take many forms: legal restrictions promulgated by a government authority, self-_____, social _____, co-_____ and market _____. One can consider _____ as actions of conduct imposing sanctions (such as a fine.) This action of administrative law, or implementing regulatory law, may be contrasted with statutory or case law.

a. CAN-SPAM
b. Rule of four
c. Non-conventional trademark
d. Regulation

8. In marketing, _____ has come to mean the process by which marketers try to create an image or identity in the minds of their target market for its product, brand, or organization. It is the 'relative competitive comparison' their product occupies in a given market as perceived by the target market.

Chapter 10. Product Adaptation

Re-_____ involves changing the identity of a product, relative to the identity of competing products, in the collective minds of the target market.

a. GE matrix
b. Containerization
c. Moratorium
d. Positioning

9. _____s is the social science that studies the production, distribution, and consumption of goods and services. The term _____s comes from the Ancient Greek oá¼°κονομῖα from oá¼¶κος (oikos, 'house') + vÏŒμος (nomos, 'custom' or 'law'), hence 'rules of the house(hold)'. Current _____ models developed out of the broader field of political economy in the late 19th century, owing to a desire to use an empirical approach more akin to the physical sciences.

a. Industrial organization
b. Economic
c. ACNielsen
d. ADTECH

10. Competitiveness is a comparative concept of the ability and performance of a firm, sub-sector or country to sell and supply goods and/or services in a given market. Although widely used in economics and business management, the usefulness of the concept, particularly in the context of national competitiveness, is vigorously disputed by economists, such as Paul Krugman .

The term may also be applied to markets, where it is used to refer to the extent to which the market structure may be regarded as perfectly _____.

a. Free trade zone
b. Customs union
c. Competitive
d. Geographical pricing

11. _____ is an organizational lifecycle function within a company dealing with the planning or marketing of a product or products at all stages of the product lifecycle.

_____ and product marketing (outbound focused) are different yet complementary efforts with the objective of maximizing sales revenues, market share, and profit margins. The role of _____ spans many activities from strategic to tactical and varies based on the organizational structure of the company.

Chapter 10. Product Adaptation

a. Service product management
b. Product management
c. Requirement prioritization
d. Product information management

12. _____ is one of the four elements of marketing mix. An organization or set of organizations (go-betweens) involved in the process of making a product or service available for use or consumption by a consumer or business user.

The other three parts of the marketing mix are product, pricing, and promotion.

a. Better Living Through Chemistry
b. Comparison-Shopping agent
c. Distribution
d. Japan Advertising Photographers' Association

13. A supply chain is the system of organizations, people, technology, activities, information and resources involved in moving a product or service from _____ to customer. Supply chain activities transform natural resources, raw materials and components into a finished product that is delivered to the end customer. In sophisticated supply chain systems, used products may re-enter the supply chain at any point where residual value is recyclable.
a. Bringin' Home the Oil
b. Rebate
c. Product line extension
d. Supplier

14. In economics, an externality or spillover of an economic transaction is an impact on a party that is not directly involved in the transaction. In such a case, prices do not reflect the full costs or benefits in production or consumption of a product or service. A positive impact is called an _____ benefit, while a negative impact is called an _____ cost.
a. ADTECH
b. AMAX
c. ACNielsen
d. External

15. A _____ product is an imitation which infringes upon a production monopoly held by either a state or corporation. Goods are produced with the intent to bypass this monopoly and thus take advantage of the established worth of the previous product. The word _____ frequently describes both the forgeries of currency and documents, as well as the imitations of clothing, software, pharmaceuticals, watches, electronics, and company logos and brands.

Chapter 10. Product Adaptation

a. 6-3-5 Brainwriting
b. Power III
c. 180SearchAssistant
d. Counterfeit

16. _____ are legal property rights over creations of the mind, both artistic and commercial, and the corresponding fields of law. Under _____ law, owners are granted certain exclusive rights to a variety of intangible assets, such as musical, literary, and artistic works; ideas, discoveries and inventions; and words, phrases, symbols, and designs. Common types of _____ include copyrights, trademarks, patents, industrial design rights and trade secrets.

a. ACNielsen
b. Opinion leadership
c. Elasticity
d. Intellectual property

17. Human beings are also considered to be _____ because they have the ability to change raw materials into valuable _____. The term Human _____ can also be defined as the skills, energies, talents, abilities and knowledge that are used for the production of goods or the rendering of services. While taking into account human beings as _____, the following things have to be kept in mind:

- The size of the population
- The capabilities of the individuals in that population

Many _____ cannot be consumed in their original form. They have to be processed in order to change them into more usable commodities.

a. 180SearchAssistant
b. Resources
c. 6-3-5 Brainwriting
d. Power III

Chapter 11. Export Pricing

1. In economics, an _____ is any good or commodity, transported from one country to another country in a legitimate fashion, typically for use in trade. _____ goods or services are provided to foreign consumers by domestic producers. _____ is an important part of international trade.

   a. AMAX
   b. Export
   c. ACNielsen
   d. ADTECH

2. The Oxford University Press defines _____ as 'marketing on a worldwide scale reconciling or taking commercial advantage of global operational differences, similarities and opportunities in order to meet global objectives.' Oxford University Press' Glossary of Marketing Terms.

   Here are three reasons for the shift from domestic to _____ as given by the authors of the textbook, _____ Management--3rd Edition by Masaaki Kotabe and Kristiaan Helsen, 2004.

   One of the product categories in which global competition has been easy to track is in U.S. automotive sales.

   a. Diversity marketing
   b. Global marketing
   c. Digital marketing
   d. Guerrilla Marketing

3. _____ is defined by the American _____ Association as the activity, set of institutions, and processes for creating, communicating, delivering, and exchanging offerings that have value for customers, clients, partners, and society at large. The term developed from the original meaning which referred literally to going to market, as in shopping, or going to a market to sell goods or services.

   _____ practice tends to be seen as a creative industry, which includes advertising, distribution and selling.

   a. Product naming
   b. Marketing myopia
   c. Customer acquisition management
   d. Marketing

4. _____ is one of the four Ps of the marketing mix. The other three aspects are product, promotion, and place. It is also a key variable in microeconomic price allocation theory.

a. Competitor indexing
b. Price
c. Relationship based pricing
d. Pricing

5. A _____ is a collection of symbols, experiences and associations connected with a product, a service, a person or any other artifact or entity.

_____s have become increasingly important components of culture and the economy, now being described as 'cultural accessories and personal philosophies'.

Some people distinguish the psychological aspect of a _____ from the experiential aspect.

a. Brand equity
b. Store brand
c. Brandable software
d. Brand

6. _____ is an organizational lifecycle function within a company dealing with the planning or marketing of a product or products at all stages of the product lifecycle.

_____ and product marketing (outbound focused) are different yet complementary efforts with the objective of maximizing sales revenues, market share, and profit margins. The role of _____ spans many activities from strategic to tactical and varies based on the organizational structure of the company.

a. Service product management
b. Product management
c. Requirement prioritization
d. Product information management

7. In economics, business, retail, and accounting, a _____ is the value of money that has been used up to produce something, and hence is not available for use anymore. In economics, a _____ is an alternative that is given up as a result of a decision. In business, the _____ may be one of acquisition, in which case the amount of money expended to acquire it is counted as _____.

a. Fixed costs
b. Cost
c. Transaction cost
d. Variable cost

Chapter 11. Export Pricing

8. _____ is one of the four elements of marketing mix. An organization or set of organizations (go-betweens) involved in the process of making a product or service available for use or consumption by a consumer or business user.

The other three parts of the marketing mix are product, pricing, and promotion.

   a. Better Living Through Chemistry
   b. Comparison-Shopping agent
   c. Japan Advertising Photographers' Association
   d. Distribution

9. _____ or international commercial terms are a series of international sales terms widely used throughout the world. They are used to divide transaction costs and responsibilities between buyer and seller and reflect state-of-the-art transportation practices. They closely correspond to the U.N. Convention on Contracts for the International Sale of Goods.
   a. ADTECH
   b. Incoterms
   c. International trade
   d. ACNielsen

10. _____ is the practice of managing the flow of information between an organization and its publics. _____ - often referred to as _____ - gains an organization or individual exposure to their audiences using topics of public interest and news items that do not require direct payment. Because _____ places exposure in credible third-party outlets, it offers a third-party legitimacy that advertising does not have.
    a. Symbolic analysis
    b. Power III
    c. Public relations
    d. Graphic communication

11. _____ is the act of consigning, which is placing a person or thing in the hand of another, but retaining ownership until the goods are sold or person is transferred. This may be done for shipping, transfer of prisoners, or for sale in a store (i.e. a _____ shop.)

Features of _____ are as follows: 1)The Relation between the two parties is that of consignor and consignee and not that of buyer and seller 2)The consignor is entitled to receive all the expenses in connection with _____ 3)The consignee is not responsible for damage of goods during transport or any other procedure.

a. History of pawnbroking
b. Self service
c. Garage sale
d. Consignment

12. _____ is an advertisement in which a particular product specifically mentions a competitor by name for the express purpose of showing why the competitor is inferior to the product naming it.

This should not be confused with parody advertisements, where a fictional product is being advertised for the purpose of poking fun at the particular advertisement, nor should it be confused with the use of a coined brand name for the purpose of comparing the product without actually naming an actual competitor. ('Wikipedia tastes better and is less filling than the Encyclopedia Galactica.')

In the 1980s, during what has been referred to as the cola wars, soft-drink manufacturer Pepsi ran a series of advertisements where people, caught on hidden camera, in a blind taste test, chose Pepsi over rival Coca-Cola.

a. Heavy-up
b. Comparative advertising
c. Cost per conversion
d. GL-70

13. Foreign _____ in its classic form is defined as a company from one country making a physical investment into building a factory in another country. It is the establishment of an enterprise by a foreigner. Its definition can be extended to include investments made to acquire lasting interest in enterprises operating outside of the economy of the investor.
a. Brash Brands
b. Fountain Fresh International
c. Direct investment
d. VideoJug

14. _____ is a concept that denotes the precise probability of specific eventualities. Technically, the notion of _____ is independent from the notion of value and, as such, eventualities may have both beneficial and adverse consequences. However, in general usage the convention is to focus only on potential negative impact to some characteristic of value that may arise from a future event.
a. 180SearchAssistant
b. Power III
c. 6-3-5 Brainwriting
d. Risk

Chapter 11. Export Pricing

15. _____ are duties imposed under WTO Rules to neutralize the negative effects of other duties. They are imposed when a foreign country subsidizes its exports, hurting domestic producers in the importing country
    a. Gray market
    b. Grey market
    c. Geographical pricing
    d. Countervailing duties

16. In economics, '_____' can refer to any kind of predatory pricing. However, the word is now generally used only in the context of international trade law, where _____ is defined as the act of a manufacturer in one country exporting a product to another country at a price which is either below the price it charges in its home market or is below its costs of production. The term has a negative connotation, but advocates of free markets see '_____' as beneficial for consumers and believe that protectionism to prevent it would have net negative consequences.
    a. Hawkers
    b. Sample sales
    c. Gold Key Matching Service
    d. Dumping

17. A _____ is a type of wholesale merchant business that buys goods and bulk products from importers, other wholesalers and then sells to retailers. _____s can deal in any commodity destined for the retail market. Typical categories are food, lumber, hardware, fuel, and textiles.
    a. Jobbing house
    b. Refusal to deal
    c. Tacit collusion
    d. Chief privacy officer

Chapter 12. Marketing Communication

1. In economics, an _____ is any good or commodity, transported from one country to another country in a legitimate fashion, typically for use in trade. _____ goods or services are provided to foreign consumers by domestic producers. _____ is an important part of international trade.

   a. ACNielsen
   b. AMAX
   c. ADTECH
   d. Export

2. The Oxford University Press defines _____ as 'marketing on a worldwide scale reconciling or taking commercial advantage of global operational differences, similarities and opportunities in order to meet global objectives.' Oxford University Press' Glossary of Marketing Terms.

   Here are three reasons for the shift from domestic to _____ as given by the authors of the textbook, _____ Management--3rd Edition by Masaaki Kotabe and Kristiaan Helsen, 2004.

   One of the product categories in which global competition has been easy to track is in U.S. automotive sales.

   a. Digital marketing
   b. Diversity marketing
   c. Guerrilla Marketing
   d. Global marketing

3. _____ is defined by the American _____ Association as the activity, set of institutions, and processes for creating, communicating, delivering, and exchanging offerings that have value for customers, clients, partners, and society at large. The term developed from the original meaning which referred literally to going to market, as in shopping, or going to a market to sell goods or services.

   _____ practice tends to be seen as a creative industry, which includes advertising, distribution and selling.

   a. Customer acquisition management
   b. Marketing myopia
   c. Product naming
   d. Marketing

4. A _____ is the space, actual or metaphorical, in which a market operates. The term is also used in a trademark law context to denote the actual consumer environment, ie. the 'real world' in which products and services are provided and consumed.

Chapter 12. Marketing Communication

a. 6-3-5 Brainwriting
b. 180SearchAssistant
c. Power III
d. Marketplace

5. _____ is the reverse of encoding, which is the process of transforming information from one format into another. Information about _____ can be found in the following:

- Digital-to-analog converter, the use of analog circuit for _____ operations
- Code, a rule for converting a piece of information into another form or representation
- Code (cryptography), a method used to transform a message into an obscured form
- _____
- _____ methods, methods in communication theory for _____ codewords sent over a noisy channel
- Digital signal processing, the study of signals in a digital representation and the processing methods of these signals
- Word _____, the use of phonics to decipher print patterns and translate them into the sounds of language
- deCODE genetics

a. Power III
b. Decoding
c. 180SearchAssistant
d. 6-3-5 Brainwriting

6. _____ describes the situation when output from (or information about the result of) an event or phenomenon in the past will influence the same event/phenomenon in the present or future. When an event is part of a chain of cause-and-effect that forms a circuit or loop, then the event is said to 'feed back' into itself.

_____ is also a synonym for:

- _____ Signal; the information about the initial event that is the basis for subsequent modification of the event.
- _____ Loop; the causal path that leads from the initial generation of the _____ signal to the subsequent modification of the event.

_____ is a mechanism, process or signal that is looped back to control a system within itself. Such a loop is called a _____ loop.

a. Power III
b. 180SearchAssistant
c. 6-3-5 Brainwriting
d. Feedback

7. _____ refers to messages and related media used to communicate with a market. Those who practice advertising, branding, direct marketing, graphic design, marketing, packaging, promotion, publicity, sponsorship, public relations, sales, sales promotion and online marketing are termed marketing communicators, _____ managers, or more briefly as marcom managers.

a. Merchandise
b. Sales promotion
c. Merchandising
d. Marketing communication

8. _____ , according to The American Marketing Association, is 'a planning process designed to assure that all brand contacts received by a customer or prospect for a product, service, or organization are relevant to that person and consistent over time.' (Marketing Power Dictionary)

_____ is a term used to describe a holistic approach to marketing. It aims to ensure consistency of message and the complementary use of media. The concept includes online and offline marketing channels.

a. ACNielsen
b. ADTECH
c. AMAX
d. Integrated marketing communications

9. The business terms _____ and pull originated in the logistic and supply chain management, but are also widely used in marketing.

A _____-pull-system in business describes the move of a product or information between two subjects. On markets the consumers usually 'pulls' the goods or information they demand for their needs, while the offerers or suppliers '_____es' them toward the consumers.

a. Gold Key Matching Service
b. Push
c. Manufacturers' representatives
d. Completely randomized designs

Chapter 12. Marketing Communication 61

10. The _____ is an English-language international daily newspaper published by Dow Jones ' Company in New York City with Asian and European editions. As of 2007, It has a worldwide daily circulation of more than 2 million, with approximately 931,000 paying online subscribers. It was the largest-circulation newspaper in the United States until November 2003, when it was surpassed by USA Today.
   a. 6-3-5 Brainwriting
   b. Power III
   c. 180SearchAssistant
   d. Wall Street Journal

11. _____s is the social science that studies the production, distribution, and consumption of goods and services. The term _____s comes from the Ancient Greek oá¼°κονομῖα from oá¼¶κος (oikos, 'house') + vĭŒμος (nomos, 'custom' or 'law'), hence 'rules of the house(hold)'. Current _____ models developed out of the broader field of political economy in the late 19th century, owing to a desire to use an empirical approach more akin to the physical sciences.
   a. Industrial organization
   b. ACNielsen
   c. ADTECH
   d. Economic

12. _____ is a term used to describe how different aspects between economies are integrated. The basics of this theory were written by the Hungarian Economist Béla Balassa in the 1960s. As _____ increases, the barriers of trade between markets diminishes.
   a. ADTECH
   b. ACNielsen
   c. Economic integration
   d. Incoterms

13. _____ is a sub-discipline and type of marketing. There are two main definitional characteristics which distinguish it from other types of marketing. The first is that it attempts to send its messages directly to consumers, without the use of intervening media.
   a. Direct Marketing Associations
   b. Power III
   c. Database marketing
   d. Direct marketing

14. A _____ is a structured collection of records or data that is stored in a computer system. The structure is achieved by organizing the data according to a _____ model. The model in most common use today is the relational model.

a. 6-3-5 Brainwriting
b. 180SearchAssistant
c. Power III
d. Database

15. _____ is a form of direct marketing using databases of customers or potential customers to generate personalized communications in order to promote a product or service for marketing purposes. The method of communication can be any addressable medium, as in direct marketing.

The distinction between direct and _____ stems primarily from the attention paid to the analysis of data.

a. Database marketing
b. Direct marketing
c. Direct Marketing Associations
d. Power III

16. A trade fair (trade show or expo) is an exhibition organized so that companies in a specific industry can showcase and demonstrate their latest products, service, study activities of rivals and examine recent trends and opportunities. Some trade fairs are open to the public, while others can only be attended by company representatives (members of the trade) and members of the press, therefore _____ are classified as either 'Public' or 'Trade Only'. They are held on a continuing basis in virtually all markets and normally attract companies from around the globe.

a. 180SearchAssistant
b. Power III
c. 6-3-5 Brainwriting
d. Trade shows

17. Human beings are also considered to be _____ because they have the ability to change raw materials into valuable _____. The term Human _____ can also be defined as the skills, energies, talents, abilities and knowledge that are used for the production of goods or the rendering of services. While taking into account human beings as _____, the following things have to be kept in mind:

- The size of the population
- The capabilities of the individuals in that population

Many _____ cannot be consumed in their original form. They have to be processed in order to change them into more usable commodities.

a. Power III
b. 180SearchAssistant
c. 6-3-5 Brainwriting
d. Resources

Chapter 13. Distribution Management

1. _____ is one of the four elements of marketing mix. An organization or set of organizations (go-betweens) involved in the process of making a product or service available for use or consumption by a consumer or business user.

The other three parts of the marketing mix are product, pricing, and promotion.

   a. Distribution
   b. Better Living Through Chemistry
   c. Japan Advertising Photographers' Association
   d. Comparison-Shopping agent

2. In economics, an _____ is any good or commodity, transported from one country to another country in a legitimate fashion, typically for use in trade. _____ goods or services are provided to foreign consumers by domestic producers. _____ is an important part of international trade.
   a. ACNielsen
   b. AMAX
   c. ADTECH
   d. Export

3. The Oxford University Press defines _____ as 'marketing on a worldwide scale reconciling or taking commercial advantage of global operational differences, similarities and opportunities in order to meet global objectives.' Oxford University Press' Glossary of Marketing Terms.

Here are three reasons for the shift from domestic to _____ as given by the authors of the textbook, _____ Management--3rd Edition by Masaaki Kotabe and Kristiaan Helsen, 2004.

One of the product categories in which global competition has been easy to track is in U.S. automotive sales.

   a. Guerrilla Marketing
   b. Digital marketing
   c. Diversity marketing
   d. Global marketing

4. _____ is defined by the American _____ Association as the activity, set of institutions, and processes for creating, communicating, delivering, and exchanging offerings that have value for customers, clients, partners, and society at large. The term developed from the original meaning which referred literally to going to market, as in shopping, or going to a market to sell goods or services.

_____ practice tends to be seen as a creative industry, which includes advertising, distribution and selling.

a. Marketing myopia
b. Customer acquisition management
c. Product naming
d. Marketing

5. A _____ is the space, actual or metaphorical, in which a market operates. The term is also used in a trademark law context to denote the actual consumer environment, ie. the 'real world' in which products and services are provided and consumed.
   a. 180SearchAssistant
   b. Power III
   c. 6-3-5 Brainwriting
   d. Marketplace

6. _____ is difficult to define. For example, in 1952, Alfred Kroeber and Clyde Kluckhohn compiled a list of 164 definitions of '_____' in _____: A Critical Review of Concepts and Definitions. However, the word '_____' is most commonly used in three basic senses:

   - excellence of taste in the fine arts and humanities
   - an integrated pattern of human knowledge, belief, and behavior that depends upon the capacity for symbolic thought and social learning
   - the set of shared attitudes, values, goals, and practices that characterizes an institution, organization or group.

   When the concept first emerged in eighteenth- and nineteenth-century Europe, it connoted a process of cultivation or improvement, as in agriculture or horticulture. In the nineteenth century, it came to refer first to the betterment or refinement of the individual, especially through education, and then to the fulfillment of national aspirations or ideals.

   a. African Americans
   b. Albert Einstein
   c. Culture
   d. AStore

7. _____ is a rivalry between individuals, groups, nations for territory, a niche, or allocation of resources. It arises whenever two or more parties strive for a goal which cannot be shared. _____ occurs naturally between living organisms which co-exist in the same environment.

a. Price fixing
b. Competition
c. Non-price competition
d. Price competition

8. In economics, business, retail, and accounting, a _____ is the value of money that has been used up to produce something, and hence is not available for use anymore. In economics, a _____ is an alternative that is given up as a result of a decision. In business, the _____ may be one of acquisition, in which case the amount of money expended to acquire it is counted as _____.
   a. Variable cost
   b. Cost
   c. Transaction cost
   d. Fixed costs

9. A grey market or _____ is the trade of a commodity through distribution channels which, while legal, are unofficial, unauthorized, or unintended by the original manufacturer. In contrast, a black market is the trade of goods and services that are illegal in themselves and/or distributed through illegal channels, such as the selling of stolen goods or illegal items such as heroin or unregistered handguns.

The two main types of grey market are imported manufactured goods that would be normally unavailable or more expensive in a certain country and unissued securities that are not yet traded in official markets.

   a. Gray market
   b. Zone pricing
   c. Green market
   d. Customs union

10. _____ is an authority or agency in a country responsible for collecting and safeguarding _____ duties and for controlling the flow of goods including animals, personal effects and hazardous items in and out of a country. Depending on local legislation and regulations, the import or export of some goods may be restricted or forbidden, and the _____ agency enforces these rules. The _____ agency may be different from the immigration authority, which monitors persons who leave or enter the country, checking for appropriate documentation, apprehending people wanted by international arrest warrants, and impeding the entry of others deemed dangerous to the country.
    a. Registered trademark symbol
    b. Specific Performance
    c. Customs
    d. Madrid system for the international registration of marks

Chapter 13. Distribution Management

11. _____ is an advertisement in which a particular product specifically mentions a competitor by name for the express purpose of showing why the competitor is inferior to the product naming it.

This should not be confused with parody advertisements, where a fictional product is being advertised for the purpose of poking fun at the particular advertisement, nor should it be confused with the use of a coined brand name for the purpose of comparing the product without actually naming an actual competitor. ('Wikipedia tastes better and is less filling than the Encyclopedia Galactica.')

In the 1980s, during what has been referred to as the cola wars, soft-drink manufacturer Pepsi ran a series of advertisements where people, caught on hidden camera, in a blind taste test, chose Pepsi over rival Coca-Cola.

   a. GL-70
   b. Heavy-up
   c. Cost per conversion
   d. Comparative advertising

12. Electronic commerce, commonly known as _____ or eCommerce, consists of the buying and selling of products or services over electronic systems such as the Internet and other computer networks. The amount of trade conducted electronically has grown extraordinarily with wide-spread Internet usage. A wide variety of commerce is conducted in this way, spurring and drawing on innovations in electronic funds transfer, supply chain management, Internet marketing, online transaction processing, electronic data interchange (EDI), inventory management systems, and automated data collection systems.
   a. ADTECH
   b. ACNielsen
   c. AMAX
   d. E-commerce

13. _____ is the practice of managing the flow of information between an organization and its publics. _____ - often referred to as _____ - gains an organization or individual exposure to their audiences using topics of public interest and news items that do not require direct payment. Because _____ places exposure in credible third-party outlets, it offers a third-party legitimacy that advertising does not have.
   a. Symbolic analysis
   b. Public relations
   c. Power III
   d. Graphic communication

Chapter 13. Distribution Management

14. Human beings are also considered to be _____ because they have the ability to change raw materials into valuable _____. The term Human _____ can also be defined as the skills, energies, talents, abilities and knowledge that are used for the production of goods or the rendering of services. While taking into account human beings as _____, the following things have to be kept in mind:

    - The size of the population
    - The capabilities of the individuals in that population

Many _____ cannot be consumed in their original form. They have to be processed in order to change them into more usable commodities.

   a. 180SearchAssistant
   b. 6-3-5 Brainwriting
   c. Power III
   d. Resources

Chapter 14. Global Product Management and Branding

1. The Oxford University Press defines _____ as 'marketing on a worldwide scale reconciling or taking commercial advantage of global operational differences, similarities and opportunities in order to meet global objectives.' Oxford University Press' Glossary of Marketing Terms.

Here are three reasons for the shift from domestic to _____ as given by the authors of the textbook, _____ Management--3rd Edition by Masaaki Kotabe and Kristiaan Helsen, 2004.

One of the product categories in which global competition has been easy to track is in U.S. automotive sales.

   a. Diversity marketing
   b. Global marketing
   c. Guerrilla Marketing
   d. Digital marketing

2. _____ is defined by the American _____ Association as the activity, set of institutions, and processes for creating, communicating, delivering, and exchanging offerings that have value for customers, clients, partners, and society at large. The term developed from the original meaning which referred literally to going to market, as in shopping, or going to a market to sell goods or services.

_____ practice tends to be seen as a creative industry, which includes advertising, distribution and selling.

   a. Customer acquisition management
   b. Marketing myopia
   c. Marketing
   d. Product naming

3. A _____ is the space, actual or metaphorical, in which a market operates. The term is also used in a trademark law context to denote the actual consumer environment, ie. the 'real world' in which products and services are provided and consumed.
   a. 180SearchAssistant
   b. Marketplace
   c. 6-3-5 Brainwriting
   d. Power III

4. _____ is an organizational lifecycle function within a company dealing with the planning or marketing of a product or products at all stages of the product lifecycle.

_____ and product marketing (outbound focused) are different yet complementary efforts with the objective of maximizing sales revenues, market share, and profit margins. The role of _____ spans many activities from strategic to tactical and varies based on the organizational structure of the company.

a. Product management
b. Product information management
c. Service product management
d. Requirement prioritization

5. _____ is subcontracting a process, such as product design or manufacturing, to a third-party company. The decision to outsource is often made in the interest of lowering cost or making better use of time and energy costs, redirecting or conserving energy directed at the competencies of a particular business, or to make more efficient use of land, labor, capital, (information) technology and resources. _____ became part of the business lexicon during the 1980s.

a. Intangible assets
b. In-house
c. Outsourcing
d. ACNielsen

6. A _____ is a collection of symbols, experiences and associations connected with a product, a service, a person or any other artifact or entity.

_____s have become increasingly important components of culture and the economy, now being described as 'cultural accessories and personal philosophies'.

Some people distinguish the psychological aspect of a _____ from the experiential aspect.

a. Brand
b. Brandable software
c. Store brand
d. Brand equity

7. _____s is the social science that studies the production, distribution, and consumption of goods and services. The term _____s comes from the Ancient Greek οἰκονομία from οἶκος (oikos, 'house') + νόμος (nomos, 'custom' or 'law'), hence 'rules of the house(hold)'. Current _____ models developed out of the broader field of political economy in the late 19th century, owing to a desire to use an empirical approach more akin to the physical sciences.

a. ADTECH
b. Industrial organization
c. ACNielsen
d. Economic

Chapter 14. Global Product Management and Branding

8. _____ is a term used to describe how different aspects between economies are integrated. The basics of this theory were written by the Hungarian Economist Béla Balassa in the 1960s. As _____ increases, the barriers of trade between markets diminishes.
   a. ACNielsen
   b. ADTECH
   c. Incoterms
   d. Economic integration

9. _____ is when a large distribution channel member (usually a retailer), buys from a manufacturer in bulk and puts its own name on the product. This strategy is only practical when the retailer does very high levels of volume. The advantages to the retailer are:

   - more freedom and flexibility in pricing
   - more control over product attributes and quality
   - higher margins (or lower selling price)
   - eliminates much of the manufacturer's promotional costs

The advantages to the manufacturer are:

   - reduced promotional costs
   - stability of sales volume (at least while the contract is operative)

   - Kumar, Nirmalya; Steenkamp, Jan-Benedict E.M., Private Label Strategy - How to Meet the Store Brand Challenge. Harvard Business Press 2007

   - private label
   - brand management
   - brand
   - product management
   - marketing

   a. Customization
   b. Promotion
   c. Private branding
   d. Rural market

Chapter 14. Global Product Management and Branding

10. Human beings are also considered to be _____ because they have the ability to change raw materials into valuable _____. The term Human _____ can also be defined as the skills, energies, talents, abilities and knowledge that are used for the production of goods or the rendering of services. While taking into account human beings as _____, the following things have to be kept in mind:

    - The size of the population
    - The capabilities of the individuals in that population

Many _____ cannot be consumed in their original form. They have to be processed in order to change them into more usable commodities.

   a. 180SearchAssistant
   b. Power III
   c. Resources
   d. 6-3-5 Brainwriting

Chapter 15. Global Services

1. The Oxford University Press defines _____ as 'marketing on a worldwide scale reconciling or taking commercial advantage of global operational differences, similarities and opportunities in order to meet global objectives.' Oxford University Press' Glossary of Marketing Terms.

Here are three reasons for the shift from domestic to _____ as given by the authors of the textbook, _____ Management--3rd Edition by Masaaki Kotabe and Kristiaan Helsen, 2004.

One of the product categories in which global competition has been easy to track is in U.S. automotive sales.

   a. Guerrilla Marketing
   b. Digital marketing
   c. Diversity marketing
   d. Global marketing

2. _____ is defined by the American _____ Association as the activity, set of institutions, and processes for creating, communicating, delivering, and exchanging offerings that have value for customers, clients, partners, and society at large. The term developed from the original meaning which referred literally to going to market, as in shopping, or going to a market to sell goods or services.

_____ practice tends to be seen as a creative industry, which includes advertising, distribution and selling.

   a. Marketing myopia
   b. Product naming
   c. Customer acquisition management
   d. Marketing

3. _____ is an advertisement in which a particular product specifically mentions a competitor by name for the express purpose of showing why the competitor is inferior to the product naming it.

This should not be confused with parody advertisements, where a fictional product is being advertised for the purpose of poking fun at the particular advertisement, nor should it be confused with the use of a coined brand name for the purpose of comparing the product without actually naming an actual competitor. ('Wikipedia tastes better and is less filling than the Encyclopedia Galactica.')

In the 1980s, during what has been referred to as the cola wars, soft-drink manufacturer Pepsi ran a series of advertisements where people, caught on hidden camera, in a blind taste test, chose Pepsi over rival Coca-Cola.

a. Heavy-up
b. GL-70
c. Cost per conversion
d. Comparative advertising

4. The _____ or gross domestic income (GDI) is one of the measures of national income and output for a given country's economy. It is the total value of all final goods and services produced in a particular economy; the dollar value of all goods and services produced within a country's borders in a given year. _____ can be defined in three ways, all of which are conceptually identical.

a. Microeconomics
b. Macroeconomics
c. Leading indicator
d. Gross domestic product

5. _____ is used in marketing to describe the inability to assess the value gained from engaging in an activity using any tangible evidence. It is often used to describe services where there isn't a tangible product that the customer can purchase, that can be seen, tasted or touched.

Other key characteristics of services include perishability, inseparability and variability.

a. Inseparability
b. Automated surveys
c. Individual branding
d. Intangibility

6. In psychology, philosophy, and the cognitive sciences, _____ is the process of attaining awareness or understanding of sensory information. It is a task far more complex than was imagined in the 1950s and 1960s, when it was predicted that building perceiving machines would take about a decade, a goal which is still very far from fruition. The word _____ comes from the Latin words _____, percepio, meaning 'receiving, collecting, action of taking possession, apprehension with the mind or senses.'

_____ is one of the oldest fields in psychology.

a. 180SearchAssistant
b. Power III
c. Perception
d. Groupthink

Chapter 15. Global Services

7. A high degree of market _____ can result in disintermediation due to the buyer's increased knowledge of supply pricing.

_____ is important since it is one of the theoretical conditions required for a free market to be efficient.

Price _____ can, however, lead to higher prices, if it makes sellers reluctant to give steep discounts to certain buyers, or if it facilitates collusion.

   a. Comparison-Shopping agent
   b. Transparency
   c. Package-on-Package
   d. Spearman's rank correlation coefficient

8. _____ is a process by which government's control over businesses and individuals is reduced or eliminated. It is the removal of some governmental controls over a market. _____ does not mean elimination of laws against fraud, but eliminating or reducing government control of how business is done, thereby moving toward a more free market.
   a. Value added
   b. Power III
   c. Consumer spending
   d. Deregulation

9. _____ is systematic determination of merit, worth, and significance of something or someone using criteria against a set of standards. _____ often is used to characterize and appraise subjects of interest in a wide range of human enterprises, including the arts, criminal justice, foundations and non-profit organizations, government, health care, and other human services.

Depending on the topic of interest, there are professional groups which look to the quality and rigor of the _____ process.

   a. ACNielsen
   b. AMAX
   c. ADTECH
   d. Evaluation

10. _____ refers to 'controlling human or societal behaviour by rules or restrictions.' _____ can take many forms: legal restrictions promulgated by a government authority, self-_____, social _____, co-_____ and market _____. One can consider _____ as actions of conduct imposing sanctions (such as a fine.) This action of administrative law, or implementing regulatory law, may be contrasted with statutory or case law.

a. Rule of four
b. CAN-SPAM
c. Non-conventional trademark
d. Regulation

11. Electronic commerce, commonly known as _____ or eCommerce, consists of the buying and selling of products or services over electronic systems such as the Internet and other computer networks. The amount of trade conducted electronically has grown extraordinarily with wide-spread Internet usage. A wide variety of commerce is conducted in this way, spurring and drawing on innovations in electronic funds transfer, supply chain management, Internet marketing, online transaction processing, electronic data interchange (EDI), inventory management systems, and automated data collection systems.
    a. ACNielsen
    b. AMAX
    c. ADTECH
    d. E-commerce

12. _____s is the social science that studies the production, distribution, and consumption of goods and services. The term _____s comes from the Ancient Greek oá¼°κονομῖα from oá¼¶κος (oikos, 'house') + vÏŒμος (nomos, 'custom' or 'law'), hence 'rules of the house(hold)'. Current _____ models developed out of the broader field of political economy in the late 19th century, owing to a desire to use an empirical approach more akin to the physical sciences.
    a. Economic
    b. ACNielsen
    c. ADTECH
    d. Industrial organization

13. The _____ is an international organization designed to supervise and liberalize international trade. The _____ came into being on 1 January 1995, and is the successor to the General Agreement on Tariffs and Trade (GATT), which was created in 1947, and continued to operate for almost five decades as a de facto international organization.

The _____ deals with the rules of trade between nations at a near-global level; it is responsible for negotiating and implementing new trade agreements, and is in charge of policing member countries' adherence to all the _____ agreements, signed by the majority of the world's trading nations and ratified in their parliaments.

    a. Population Reference Bureau
    b. Merchandise Mart
    c. BSI Group
    d. World Trade Organization

Chapter 16. Global Logistics and Materials Management

1. The Oxford University Press defines _____ as 'marketing on a worldwide scale reconciling or taking commercial advantage of global operational differences, similarities and opportunities in order to meet global objectives.' Oxford University Press' Glossary of Marketing Terms.

Here are three reasons for the shift from domestic to _____ as given by the authors of the textbook, _____ Management--3rd Edition by Masaaki Kotabe and Kristiaan Helsen, 2004.

One of the product categories in which global competition has been easy to track is in U.S. automotive sales.

   a. Diversity marketing
   b. Guerrilla Marketing
   c. Digital marketing
   d. Global marketing

2. _____ is the management of the flow of goods, information and other resources, including energy and people, between the point of origin and the point of consumption in order to meet the requirements of consumers (frequently, and originally, military organizations.) _____ involves the integration of information, transportation, inventory, warehousing, material-handling, and packaging. _____ is a channel of the supply chain which adds the value of time and place utility.
   a. Power III
   b. 6-3-5 Brainwriting
   c. Logistics
   d. 180SearchAssistant

3. _____ is defined by the American _____ Association as the activity, set of institutions, and processes for creating, communicating, delivering, and exchanging offerings that have value for customers, clients, partners, and society at large. The term developed from the original meaning which referred literally to going to market, as in shopping, or going to a market to sell goods or services.

_____ practice tends to be seen as a creative industry, which includes advertising, distribution and selling.

   a. Marketing myopia
   b. Product naming
   c. Customer acquisition management
   d. Marketing

4. _____ is the branch of logistics that deals with the tangible components of a supply chain. Specifically, this covers the acquisition of spare parts and replacements, quality control of purchasing and ordering such parts, and the standards involved in ordering, shipping, and warehousing the said parts.

A large component of _____ is ensuring that parts and materials used in the supply chain meet minimum requirements by performing quality assurance (QA.)

Chapter 16. Global Logistics and Materials Management

   a. Customer driven supply chain
   b. Reverse auction
   c. Vendor Managed Inventory
   d. Materials management

5. _____ refer to a collection of facts usually collected as the result of experience, observation or experiment or a set of premises. This may consist of numbers, words particularly as measurements or observations of a set of variables. _____ are often viewed as a lowest level of abstraction from which information and knowledge are derived.

   a. Pearson product-moment correlation coefficient
   b. Mean
   c. Sample size
   d. Data

6. _____ is an advertisement in which a particular product specifically mentions a competitor by name for the express purpose of showing why the competitor is inferior to the product naming it.

This should not be confused with parody advertisements, where a fictional product is being advertised for the purpose of poking fun at the particular advertisement, nor should it be confused with the use of a coined brand name for the purpose of comparing the product without actually naming an actual competitor. ('Wikipedia tastes better and is less filling than the Encyclopedia Galactica.')

In the 1980s, during what has been referred to as the cola wars, soft-drink manufacturer Pepsi ran a series of advertisements where people, caught on hidden camera, in a blind taste test, chose Pepsi over rival Coca-Cola.

   a. Comparative advertising
   b. GL-70
   c. Heavy-up
   d. Cost per conversion

7. The United States _____ is the government agency that is responsible for the United States Census. It also gathers other national demographic and economic data.

   a. 6-3-5 Brainwriting
   b. Census Bureau
   c. 180SearchAssistant
   d. Power III

Chapter 16. Global Logistics and Materials Management

8. In economics, an _____ is any good or commodity, transported from one country to another country in a legitimate fashion, typically for use in trade. _____ goods or services are provided to foreign consumers by domestic producers. _____ is an important part of international trade.
   a. ADTECH
   b. AMAX
   c. ACNielsen
   d. Export

9. A _____ is a party that mediates between a buyer and a seller. A _____ who also acts as a seller or as a buyer becomes a principal party to the deal. Distinguish agent: one who acts on behalf of a principal.
   a. 180SearchAssistant
   b. Power III
   c. Spokesperson
   d. Broker

10. _____ is an authority or agency in a country responsible for collecting and safeguarding _____ duties and for controlling the flow of goods including animals, personal effects and hazardous items in and out of a country. Depending on local legislation and regulations, the import or export of some goods may be restricted or forbidden, and the _____ agency enforces these rules. The _____ agency may be different from the immigration authority, which monitors persons who leave or enter the country, checking for appropriate documentation, apprehending people wanted by international arrest warrants, and impeding the entry of others deemed dangerous to the country.
    a. Madrid system for the international registration of marks
    b. Customs
    c. Registered trademark symbol
    d. Specific Performance

11. The verb _____ or grant _____ means to give permission. The noun _____ refers to that permission as well as to the document memorializing that permission. _____ may be granted by a party to another party as an element of an agreement between those parties.
    a. Power III
    b. License
    c. 6-3-5 Brainwriting
    d. 180SearchAssistant

12. In marketing, _____ refers to the total cost of holding inventory. This includes warehousing costs such as rent, utilities and salaries, financial costs such as opportunity cost, and inventory costs related to perishability, shrinkage and insurance.

When there are no transaction costs for shipment, _____s are minimized when no excess inventory is held at all, as in a Just In Time production system.

a. Merchandise management system
b. Carrying cost
c. Vendor Managed Inventory
d. Reverse auction

13. In economics, business, retail, and accounting, a _____ is the value of money that has been used up to produce something, and hence is not available for use anymore. In economics, a _____ is an alternative that is given up as a result of a decision. In business, the _____ may be one of acquisition, in which case the amount of money expended to acquire it is counted as _____.

a. Fixed costs
b. Transaction cost
c. Variable cost
d. Cost

14. _____ is the provision of service to customers before, during and after a purchase.

According to Turban et al., '_____ is a series of activities designed to enhance the level of customer satisfaction - that is, the feeling that a product or service has met the customer expectation.'

Its importance varies by product, industry and customer.

a. Customer experience
b. COPC Inc.
c. Facing
d. Customer service

15. _____ measures the performance of a system. Certain goals are defined and the _____ gives the percentage to which they should be achieved.

Examples

- Percentage of calls answered in a call center.
- Percentage of customers waiting less than a given fixed time.
- Percentage of customers that do not experience a stock out.

Chapter 16. Global Logistics and Materials Management

_____ is used in supply chain management and in inventory management to measure the performance of inventory systems.

Under stochastic conditions it is unavoidable that in some periods the inventory on hand is not sufficient to deliver the complete demand and, as a consequence, that part of the demand is filled only after an inventory-related waiting time.

a. False designation of origin
b. Nielsen SoundScan
c. Symbol group
d. Service level

16. A _____ is a customs union with common policies on product regulation, and freedom of movement of the factors of production (capital and labour) and of enterprise. The goal is that the movement of capital, labour, goods, and services between the members is as easy as within them. This is the fourth stage of economic integration.
a. Monetary union
b. Customs union
c. Common Market
d. Competitive

Chapter 17. Global Pricing

1. The Oxford University Press defines _____ as 'marketing on a worldwide scale reconciling or taking commercial advantage of global operational differences, similarities and opportunities in order to meet global objectives.' Oxford University Press' Glossary of Marketing Terms.

   Here are three reasons for the shift from domestic to _____ as given by the authors of the textbook, _____ Management--3rd Edition by Masaaki Kotabe and Kristiaan Helsen, 2004.

   One of the product categories in which global competition has been easy to track is in U.S. automotive sales.

   a. Digital marketing
   b. Global marketing
   c. Guerrilla Marketing
   d. Diversity marketing

2. _____ is defined by the American _____ Association as the activity, set of institutions, and processes for creating, communicating, delivering, and exchanging offerings that have value for customers, clients, partners, and society at large. The term developed from the original meaning which referred literally to going to market, as in shopping, or going to a market to sell goods or services.

   _____ practice tends to be seen as a creative industry, which includes advertising, distribution and selling.

   a. Marketing
   b. Customer acquisition management
   c. Product naming
   d. Marketing myopia

3. _____ is one of the four Ps of the marketing mix. The other three aspects are product, promotion, and place. It is also a key variable in microeconomic price allocation theory.
   a. Relationship based pricing
   b. Competitor indexing
   c. Pricing
   d. Price

4. In economics, business, retail, and accounting, a _____ is the value of money that has been used up to produce something, and hence is not available for use anymore. In economics, a _____ is an alternative that is given up as a result of a decision. In business, the _____ may be one of acquisition, in which case the amount of money expended to acquire it is counted as _____.

Chapter 17. Global Pricing

a. Fixed costs
b. Transaction cost
c. Variable cost
d. Cost

5. In economics, an externality or spillover of an economic transaction is an impact on a party that is not directly involved in the transaction. In such a case, prices do not reflect the full costs or benefits in production or consumption of a product or service. A positive impact is called an _____ benefit, while a negative impact is called an _____ cost.

a. ADTECH
b. External
c. AMAX
d. ACNielsen

6. In economics, _____ is the desire to own something and the ability to pay for it. The term _____ signifies the ability or the willingness to buy a particular commodity at a given point of time .

a. Market dominance
b. Market system
c. Discretionary spending
d. Demand

7. _____ is the process by which an organization deals with any major unpredictable event that threatens to harm the organization, its stakeholders, or the general public. Three elements are common to most definitions of crisis: (a) a threat to the organization, (b) the element of surprise, and (c) a short decision time.

Whereas risk management involves assessing potential threats and finding the best ways to avoid those threats, _____ involves dealing with the disasters after they have occurred.

a. Performance measurement
b. Product marketing
c. Voice of the customer
d. Crisis management

8. _____ in economics and business is the result of an exchange and from that trade we assign a numerical monetary value to a good, service or asset. If I trade 4 apples for an orange, the _____ of an orange is 4 - apples. Inversely, the _____ of an apple is 1/4 oranges.

Chapter 17. Global Pricing

   a. Price
   b. Contribution margin-based pricing
   c. Discounts and allowances
   d. Pricing

9. _____ is a broad label that refers to any individuals or households that use goods and services generated within the economy. The concept of a _____ is used in different contexts, so that the usage and significance of the term may vary.

A _____ is a person who uses any product or service.

   a. 6-3-5 Brainwriting
   b. Power III
   c. 180SearchAssistant
   d. Consumer

10. _____ is exchanging goods or services that are paid for, in whole or part, with other goods or services.

There are five main variants of _____:

   - Barter: Exchange of goods or services directly for other goods or services without the use of money as means of purchase or payment.
   - Switch trading: Practice in which one company sells to another its obligation to make a purchase in a given country.
   - Counter purchase: Sale of goods and services to a country by a company that promises to make a future purchase of a specific product from the country.
   - Buyback: occurs when a firm builds a plant in a country - or supplies technology, equipment, training, or other services to the country and agrees to take a certain percentage of the plant's output as partial payment for the contract.
   - Offset: Agreement that a company will offset a hard - currency purchase of an unspecified product from that nation in the future. Agreement by one nation to buy a product from another, subject to the purchase of some or all of the components and raw materials from the buyer of the finished product, or the assembly of such product in the buyer nation.

   a. Retail loss prevention
   b. RFM
   c. Merchant
   d. Countertrade

Chapter 18. Global Promotional Strategies

1. The Oxford University Press defines _____ as 'marketing on a worldwide scale reconciling or taking commercial advantage of global operational differences, similarities and opportunities in order to meet global objectives.' Oxford University Press' Glossary of Marketing Terms.

Here are three reasons for the shift from domestic to _____ as given by the authors of the textbook, _____ Management--3rd Edition by Masaaki Kotabe and Kristiaan Helsen, 2004.

One of the product categories in which global competition has been easy to track is in U.S. automotive sales.

   a. Global marketing
   b. Diversity marketing
   c. Guerrilla Marketing
   d. Digital marketing

2. _____ is defined by the American _____ Association as the activity, set of institutions, and processes for creating, communicating, delivering, and exchanging offerings that have value for customers, clients, partners, and society at large. The term developed from the original meaning which referred literally to going to market, as in shopping, or going to a market to sell goods or services.

_____ practice tends to be seen as a creative industry, which includes advertising, distribution and selling.

   a. Product naming
   b. Marketing myopia
   c. Customer acquisition management
   d. Marketing

3. _____ is a form of communication that typically attempts to persuade potential customers to purchase or to consume more of a particular brand of product or service. 'While now central to the contemporary global economy and the reproduction of global production networks, it is only quite recently that _____ has been more than a marginal influence on patterns of sales and production. The formation of modern _____ was intimately bound up with the emergence of new forms of monopoly capitalism around the end of the 19th century and beginning of the 20th century as one element in corporate strategies to create, organize and where possible control markets, especially for mass produced consumer goods.
   a. AMAX
   b. ADTECH
   c. Advertising
   d. ACNielsen

Chapter 18. Global Promotional Strategies

4. _____ refers to a type of marketing involving the cooperative efforts of a 'for profit' business and a non-profit organization for mutual benefit. The term is sometimes used more broadly and generally to refer to any type of marketing effort for social and other charitable causes, including in-house marketing efforts by non-profit organizations. Cause marketing differs from corporate giving (philanthropy) as the latter generally involves a specific donation that is tax deductible, while cause marketing is a marketing relationship generally not based on a donation.
   a. Diversity marketing
   b. Cause-related marketing
   c. Digital marketing
   d. Global marketing

5. _____ in organizations and public policy is both the organizational process of creating and maintaining a plan; and the psychological process of thinking about the activities required to create a desired goal on some scale. As such, it is a fundamental property of intelligent behavior. This thought process is essential to the creation and refinement of a plan, or integration of it with other plans, that is, it combines forecasting of developments with the preparation of scenarios of how to react to them.
   a. Power III
   b. 180SearchAssistant
   c. 6-3-5 Brainwriting
   d. Planning

6. In marketing and advertising, a _____ usually an advertising campaign, is aimed at appealing to. A _____ can be people of a certain age group, gender, marital status, etc. (ex: teenagers, females, single people, etc.)
   a. Brand Development Index
   b. Targeted advertising
   c. National brand
   d. Target audience

7. A _____ refers to how a corporation is perceived. It is a generally accepted image of what a company 'stands for'. The creation of a _____ is an exercise in perception management.
   a. Lifetime value
   b. Buying center
   c. Corporate image
   d. Demand generation

8. _____s is the social science that studies the production, distribution, and consumption of goods and services. The term _____s comes from the Ancient Greek oá¼°κονομῖα from oá¼¶κος (oikos, 'house') + vϊŒμος (nomos, 'custom' or 'law'), hence 'rules of the house(hold)'. Current _____ models developed out of the broader field of political economy in the late 19th century, owing to a desire to use an empirical approach more akin to the physical sciences.

Chapter 18. Global Promotional Strategies

a. ACNielsen
b. Industrial organization
c. Economic
d. ADTECH

9. _____ is a form of advertisement, where branded goods or services are placed in a context usually devoid of ads, such as movies, the story line of television shows Broadcasting ' Cable reported, 'Two thirds of advertisers employ 'branded entertainment'--_____--with the vast majority of that (80%) in commercial TV programming.' The story, based on a survey by the Association of National Advertisers, added, 'Reasons for using in-show plugs varied from 'stronger emotional connection' to better dovetailing with relevant content, to targetting a specific group.'

_____ became common in the 1980s, but can be traced back to the nineteenth century in publishing.

a. 180SearchAssistant
b. Power III
c. 6-3-5 Brainwriting
d. Product placement

10. _____ is an advertisement in which a particular product specifically mentions a competitor by name for the express purpose of showing why the competitor is inferior to the product naming it.

This should not be confused with parody advertisements, where a fictional product is being advertised for the purpose of poking fun at the particular advertisement, nor should it be confused with the use of a coined brand name for the purpose of comparing the product without actually naming an actual competitor. ('Wikipedia tastes better and is less filling than the Encyclopedia Galactica.')

In the 1980s, during what has been referred to as the cola wars, soft-drink manufacturer Pepsi ran a series of advertisements where people, caught on hidden camera, in a blind taste test, chose Pepsi over rival Coca-Cola.

a. Comparative advertising
b. Cost per conversion
c. Heavy-up
d. GL-70

11. _____ is a magazine, delivering news, analysis and data on marketing and media. The magazine was started as a broadsheet newspaper in Chicago in 1930. Today, its content appears in a print weekly distributed around the world and on many electronic platforms, including: AdAge.com, daily e-mail newsletters called Ad Age Daily, Ad Age's Mediaworks and Ad Age Digital; weekly newsletters such as Madison ' Vine (about branded entertainment) and Ad Age China; podcasts called Why It Matters and various videos.

Chapter 18. Global Promotional Strategies

a. Adweek
b. Ethical Consumer
c. Advertising Age
d. Outsert

12. A _____ is a relatively new executive level position at a corporation, company, organization typically reporting directly to the CEO or board of directors. The _____ is responsible for a brand's image, experience, and promise, and propagating it throughout all aspects of the company. The brand officer oversees marketing, advertising, design, public relations and customer service departments.

a. Financial analyst
b. Power III
c. Chief brand officer
d. Chief executive officer

13. _____ is the provision of service to customers before, during and after a purchase.

According to Turban et al., '_____ is a series of activities designed to enhance the level of customer satisfaction - that is, the feeling that a product or service has met the customer expectation.'

Its importance varies by product, industry and customer.

a. COPC Inc.
b. Facing
c. Customer experience
d. Customer service

14. A supply chain is the system of organizations, people, technology, activities, information and resources involved in moving a product or service from _____ to customer. Supply chain activities transform natural resources, raw materials and components into a finished product that is delivered to the end customer. In sophisticated supply chain systems, used products may re-enter the supply chain at any point where residual value is recyclable.

a. Rebate
b. Bringin' Home the Oil
c. Supplier
d. Product line extension

Chapter 18. Global Promotional Strategies

15. _____ is the practice of managing the flow of information between an organization and its publics. _____ - often referred to as _____ - gains an organization or individual exposure to their audiences using topics of public interest and news items that do not require direct payment. Because _____ places exposure in credible third-party outlets, it offers a third-party legitimacy that advertising does not have.
    a. Symbolic analysis
    b. Graphic communication
    c. Power III
    d. Public relations

16. In economics, an externality or spillover of an economic transaction is an impact on a party that is not directly involved in the transaction. In such a case, prices do not reflect the full costs or benefits in production or consumption of a product or service. A positive impact is called an _____ benefit, while a negative impact is called an _____ cost.
    a. AMAX
    b. ACNielsen
    c. ADTECH
    d. External

17. _____ is a marketing campaign that takes place around an event but does not involve payment of a sponsorship fee to the event. For most events of any significance, one brand will pay to become the exclusive and official sponsor of the event in a particular category or categories, and this exclusivity creates a problem for one or more other brands. Those other brands then find ways to promote themselves in connection with the same event, without paying the sponsorship fee and without breaking any laws.
    a. ACNielsen
    b. ADTECH
    c. AMAX
    d. Ambush marketing

18. _____ is a contract between two parties, one being the employer and the other being the employee. An employee may be defined as: 'A person in the service of another under any contract of hire, express or implied, oral or written, where the employer has the power or right to control and direct the employee in the material details of how the work is to be performed.' Black's Law Dictionary page 471 (5th ed. 1979.)
    a. ADTECH
    b. AMAX
    c. Employment
    d. ACNielsen

Chapter 18. Global Promotional Strategies

19. In finance, an _____ is a contract between a buyer and a seller that gives the buyer the right--but not the obligation-- to buy or to sell a particular asset (the underlying asset) at a later day at an agreed price. In return for granting the _____, the seller collects a payment (the premium) from the buyer. A call _____ gives the buyer the right to buy the underlying asset; a put _____ gives the buyer of the _____ the right to sell the underlying asset.
    a. ACNielsen
    b. AMAX
    c. ADTECH
    d. Option

20. _____ is one of the four Ps of the marketing mix. The other three aspects are product, promotion, and place. It is also a key variable in microeconomic price allocation theory.
    a. Competitor indexing
    b. Relationship based pricing
    c. Price
    d. Pricing

21. In economics, business, retail, and accounting, a _____ is the value of money that has been used up to produce something, and hence is not available for use anymore. In economics, a _____ is an alternative that is given up as a result of a decision. In business, the _____ may be one of acquisition, in which case the amount of money expended to acquire it is counted as _____.
    a. Transaction cost
    b. Cost
    c. Variable cost
    d. Fixed costs

22. Human beings are also considered to be _____ because they have the ability to change raw materials into valuable _____. The term Human _____ can also be defined as the skills, energies, talents, abilities and knowledge that are used for the production of goods or the rendering of services. While taking into account human beings as _____, the following things have to be kept in mind:

    - The size of the population
    - The capabilities of the individuals in that population

Many _____ cannot be consumed in their original form. They have to be processed in order to change them into more usable commodities.

a. 6-3-5 Brainwriting
b. Resources
c. Power III
d. 180SearchAssistant

23. _____ is an authority or agency in a country responsible for collecting and safeguarding _____ duties and for controlling the flow of goods including animals, personal effects and hazardous items in and out of a country. Depending on local legislation and regulations, the import or export of some goods may be restricted or forbidden, and the _____ agency enforces these rules. The _____ agency may be different from the immigration authority, which monitors persons who leave or enter the country, checking for appropriate documentation, apprehending people wanted by international arrest warrants, and impeding the entry of others deemed dangerous to the country.
   a. Customs
   b. Madrid system for the international registration of marks
   c. Registered trademark symbol
   d. Specific Performance

24. The _____ was the outcome of the failure of negotiating governments to create the International Trade Organization (ITO.) GATT was formed in 1947 and lasted until 1994, when it was replaced by the World Trade Organization. The Bretton Woods Conference had introduced the idea for an organization to regulate trade as part of a larger plan for economic recovery after World War II.
   a. Power III
   b. Trade pact
   c. General Agreement on Trade in Services
   d. General Agreement on Tariffs and Trade

25. A _____ is a tax imposed on goods when they are moved across a political boundary. They are usually associated with protectionism, the economic policy of restraining trade between nations. For political reasons, _____s are usually imposed on imported goods, although they may also be imposed on exported goods.
   a. Monetary policy
   b. Fiscal policy
   c. Tariff
   d. Power III

26. A _____ is a type of wholesale merchant business that buys goods and bulk products from importers, other wholesalers and then sells to retailers. _____s can deal in any commodity destined for the retail market. Typical categories are food, lumber, hardware, fuel, and textiles.

Chapter 18. Global Promotional Strategies

   a. Tacit collusion
   b. Refusal to deal
   c. Chief privacy officer
   d. Jobbing house

27. The _____ is an economic and political union of 27 member states, located primarily in Europe. It was established by the Treaty of Maastricht on 1 November 1993 upon the foundations of the pre-existing European Economic Community. With almost 500 million citizens, the _____ combined generates an estimated 30% share (US$16.8 trillion in 2007) of the nominal gross world product.
   a. ADTECH
   b. ACNielsen
   c. Eurozone
   d. European Union

ANSWER KEY

Chapter 1
    1. a   2. d   3. b   4. d   5. d   6. d   7. b

Chapter 2
    1. a   2. c   3. d   4. d   5. c   6. d   7. d   8. c   9. d

Chapter 3
    1. d   2. d   3. b   4. d   5. a   6. d   7. a   8. d   9. a   10. d
    11. b   12. a   13. d   14. d

Chapter 4
    1. d   2. a   3. b   4. d   5. b   6. c   7. d   8. c   9. d   10. d
    11. a   12. b   13. b   14. a   15. d   16. c   17. d   18. a   19. d   20. c
    21. d   22. b   23. b   24. b   25. d   26. b   27. a   28. d   29. b

Chapter 5
    1. d   2. d   3. c   4. c   5. a   6. d   7. a   8. a   9. d   10. d
    11. d   12. b   13. a   14. d   15. d   16. d

Chapter 6
    1. d   2. c   3. d   4. d   5. d   6. b   7. d   8. b   9. a   10. d
    11. d   12. a   13. d

Chapter 7
    1. d   2. d   3. d   4. d   5. d   6. d   7. d   8. d   9. d   10. d

Chapter 8
    1. a   2. d   3. a   4. d   5. c   6. a   7. d   8. d   9. d   10. b
    11. d   12. d   13. d   14. d   15. b   16. d   17. c   18. b   19. d   20. c
    21. d   22. d   23. b   24. b

Chapter 9
    1. a   2. d   3. b   4. d   5. b   6. a   7. c   8. b   9. a   10. d
    11. d   12. d   13. d   14. d   15. c   16. c   17. a   18. c

Chapter 10
    1. c   2. d   3. a   4. a   5. c   6. b   7. d   8. d   9. b   10. c
    11. b   12. c   13. d   14. d   15. d   16. d   17. b

Chapter 11
    1. b   2. b   3. d   4. d   5. d   6. b   7. b   8. d   9. b   10. c
    11. d   12. b   13. c   14. d   15. d   16. d   17. a

Chapter 12
    1. d   2. d   3. d   4. d   5. b   6. d   7. d   8. d   9. b   10. d
    11. d   12. c   13. d   14. d   15. a   16. d   17. d

ANSWER KEY

Chapter 13
1. a 2. d 3. d 4. d 5. d 6. c 7. b 8. b 9. a 10. c
11. d 12. d 13. b 14. d

Chapter 14
1. b 2. c 3. b 4. a 5. c 6. a 7. d 8. d 9. c 10. c

Chapter 15
1. d 2. d 3. d 4. d 5. d 6. c 7. b 8. d 9. d 10. d
11. d 12. a 13. d

Chapter 16
1. d 2. c 3. d 4. d 5. d 6. a 7. b 8. d 9. d 10. b
11. b 12. b 13. d 14. d 15. d 16. c

Chapter 17
1. b 2. a 3. c 4. d 5. b 6. d 7. d 8. a 9. d 10. d

Chapter 18
1. a 2. d 3. c 4. b 5. d 6. d 7. c 8. c 9. d 10. a
11. c 12. c 13. d 14. c 15. d 16. d 17. d 18. c 19. d 20. d
21. b 22. b 23. a 24. d 25. c 26. d 27. d

www.ingramcontent.com/pod-product-compliance
Lightning Source LLC
Chambersburg PA
CBHW081846230426
43669CB00018B/2842